Raised By Wolves: War of the World-Views

An Examination of Season One of the Aaron Guzikowski and Ridley Scott Show

by Ken Ammi

It's like a big haunted house, and it's about the people who lived there before, all the rooms you haven't seen the inside of, the backyard you haven't seen yet
—Aaron Guzikowski

No End Books

"…of making many books there is no end;
and much study is a weariness of the flesh.
Let us hear the conclusion of the whole matter:
Fear God, and keep his commandments:
for this is the whole duty of man."
—Ecclesiastes 12

Commencement

I decided to forego a traditional *Introduction* to my book in favor of a *Commencement* of the review so that rather than stating the obvious, such as that "I am herein reviewing this show," we could get directly into the background of the show before diving into it, episode by episode.

The combination of a script by Aaron Guzikowski, the production of Ridley Scott, and several directors (including Scott, who directed the first two episodes), has resulted in a fascinating neo-sci-fi Transhumanist mythos, and Transhumanism inevitably combines high-tech, evolution, and occultism.

I had not heard of Guzikowski before but know that Scott is an Atheist since I researched him for my book *A Worldview Review of the Alien and Predator Mythos Franchises*. I have come to learn that Guzikowski has stated:

> I was brought up Catholic, so I definitely have it knocking around in my brain anyway. I'm not a practicing Catholic, but I often make connections to Catholic iconography or Bible stories, and things like that.
>
> It's an attractive thing to layer into certain types of stories for whatever reason. There's mystery to it, and all the connotations that come along with it that are always interesting, but also it's just part of the world.[1]

Hilariously, Scott, the Atheist, stated, "The scripts that Aaron Guzikowski wrote were an inspiration...I read the show and thought, 'Oh my God. This is great.'"[2]

Both of these worldviews, Atheism and Catholicism (in a manner of speaking) come into play in *Raised by Wolves*— thus, my subtitle's reference to a *War of the World-Views*.

Thus, this is an example of something I have emphasized in my other movie and show review books: our real-life worldviews cannot help but influence and be expressed even via that which is supposed to be fiction.

The show, which is set beginning in 2145 AD, is premised upon the devastating results of a conflict between Atheists and adherents of Mithraism—pertaining to *Mithra*: no, sadly, not *Mothra*.

Guzikowski has noted, "the earth was ended by this massive religious war that was started by the Mithraic religion - which is a real religion that predates Christianity. The idea's that it came back into the fore and begin the end times, more or less."[3]

Yes, Mithraism was (unsure it still "is") a real religion but that it predates Christianity seems to not be the case: it is generally dated to have had its inception in the first, or late first, or second centuries AD.

Anti-Christian fake-cumentaries, such as *Zeitgeist*, claimed that early Christians borrowed some of Mithraism's claims and applied them to Jesus—the ol' Pagan copycat conspiracy. Of course, actual research not only debunked such claims but shows that if any borrowing was occurring, it was in the other direction. It has also been uncovered that many such claims are literal neo-mythology: claims of likenesses where there are none.[4]

Thus, the future that the show envisages sees the death of

Christianity and its replacement with one of its chief counterfeits.

Guzikowski stated:

> The Mithraic was this real cult, this real religion — but very little is known about it. You even have these things called the Mithraic mysteries, all these aspects of the religion that are really poorly understood.
>
> To me, that was the perfect way in. I wanted to find something that was real, but also, something inherently mysterious. Something that hadn't been figured out, so it could kind of play that role in the story.[5]

Reportedly, "The worshippers of Mithras were divided into seven grades, each marking a stage of knowledge in the cult's mysteries. An initiate started as Corax (the Raven)" which seems to be depicted as Ridley Scott's production company.[6]

In doing some background research for this book I found that Siddhant Adlakha touched upon something I had written within the reviews of one of the episodes:

> It is, admittedly, a little strange that the cult in question seems drawn from real-world Mithraism, an ancient Roman religion inspired by the Zoroastrian deity Mithras,

when it bears all the hallmarks of Western
Christianity through the ages…Mithraism
seen in the show is merely Christianity with
a few specifics swapped around.[7]

The show could easily be viewed as a sideline rabbit hole
to Scott's *Aliens* mythos which, of course, correlates with
his Philip K. Dick based *Blade Runner* movie (which is
based on Dick's novel *Do Androids Dream of Electric
Sheep?*).

All are premised upon mommy and daddy issues,
pregnancy issues, phallic creatures, birth through orifices
that were not designed to serve such a function, evolution,
occultism, artificial intelligence (AI), androids
(anthropomorphic robots), etc.

There is also this from Guzikowski, "When I pitched this to
Ridley, I told him that I had androids with black blood."[8]
Yet, they went with white, which is typical of Scott's *Alien*
mythos, as Scott put it, "my androids are milky white
inside…it's more uncomfortable than seeing red blood…It
also amps up the psychosexual body horrors"[9] which I will
leave un-elucidated—capiche?

Guzikowski has stated, "It's also about creators and
creations."[10] The mythos is also a Golem tale with the only
exception being that the Golem is made of metallic alloys
rather than the dust of the Earth—and yet, metallic alloys
are harvested from among the dust of the Earth—much like
Mary Shelley's *Frankenstein, or The Modern Prometheus*
is a Golem tale with the dust of the Earth being replaced by
previously living human bodies—and yet, human bodies
consist of the stuff of the dust of the Earth.

Guzikowski notes:

> …we have a multiple-season plan that will
> illuminate a lot of stuff.
> It's like a big haunted house, and it's about
> the people who lived there before, all the
> rooms you haven't seen the inside of, the
> backyard you haven't seen yet.[11]

He also noted, "Raised by Wolves…requires a lot of
thinking outside of the box"[12] and I wrote this book in
order to attempt a peek inside of that box.

Two protagonists are androids. Now, by definition androids
are anthropomorphic robots and can only be categorized as
male or female by how they are made to look and how they
are programmed to comport themselves.
This allowed Guzikowski and Scott to touch upon an aspect
that many will simply ponder on the level of gender issues
but which is ultimately occult.

The protagonists are mostly always known as *Father* and
Mother since they have been thusly programmed (or, re-
programmed—as we shall see).

Now, one frustrating thing about writing show and movie
reviews based on worldview is that 99% of that which
people discuss about such tales is irrelevant to me: the
acting, the funding, the cinematography, the this, the that,
the other.
For example, there are about 1,001 articles online about the
android's bodysuits: what they are made of, whether they
are comfortable, etc., etc., etc.

What I get from such discussion is that, as Scott put it:
> I thought: "Can I do elastic suits? Can I give
> a female an androgynous look like David
> Bowie?"

> I wanted Mother to have a short haircut, red
> hair and an elastic suit — she has this
> wonderful demeanor of placidity, but she
> could become suddenly dangerous.[13]

Androgyny and David Bowie—and Bowie's androgyny
phase—stinks of occultism. How? Well, as elucidated in
my book *The Occult Roots of Postgenderism: And a
History of Changes to Psychiatry and Psychology*: occult
texts (by any other name: witchcraft, Satanic, Luciferian,
magickal, etc., etc., etc.) are saturated by the concept that
the ultimate *god* and primal human are androgynous (or
hermaphroditic) and so the ultimate goal of humanity
should be to evolve to this state once again.

For some background on Bowie's occultism, see this
endnote.[14]

Jennifer Vineyard asked if they are "looking to hire some
female or nonbinary directors for Season 2?"[15] and we can
only hope that it does not turn into an *SJW* (a virtue-
signaling Social Justice Warrior) show such as was done
with the simply unwatchable *Lovecraft Country*.

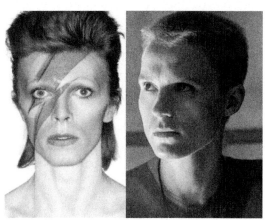

*L: David Bowie in his Ziggy Stardust persona
(featuring lightning symbolism: look
for my reference to Luke 10:18 below)*

R: Mother

Yet, Mother (and Father) is not simply androgynous but, as Guzikowski puts, it, "She represents something larger, both God and the devil, the beginning and the end."[16]

Indeed, Mother is not exactly very feminine. In describing Mother, and thus describing the real-life actress Amanda Collin—and/or visa versa—I wrote the sentence that she has the "physique of a broom handle."
I wondered how that would be taken since I was stating it as a simple fact, and then I ran across an interview with Collin herself where she described herself as, "I'm a 180 stick and obviously I was working out a lot to build muscle and not look so stick-like" thus, I was not far off—nor was I offensive, right?[17]

Why is it unacceptable, in first world country cultures, to make fun of calorically over-endowed (fat) people (fat-shaming) but perfectly acceptable to make fun of calorically underendowed (too skinny) people ("Eat a hamburger!" and such)?

Amanda Collin, who plays Mother, has stated:
>...the mother of new humanity in a skintight
>suit that doesn't have a gender and no hair -
>there's so little feminine energy about my
>look. Which I loved, because then you're
>able to just emerge that energy or whatever,
>and I think that's a beautiful point.[18]

I am unsure why she referred to "no hair" unless that was an original and then discarded concept.

She also stated:

9

I think Mother and Father have a very beautiful partnership and I think the look of the characters, two genderless robots that could be siblings, they could be lovers, they could be anything you want them to be. The whole world can relate to these people because they are just an essence of love and protection, that in itself is beautiful.

Then from then on the dynamics they have, when Mother gains more power and what is power, what is empathy, what is coming of age with children and how do you support that in the best possible way? These aren't questions for the current time, they're questions that exist in all times.[19]

As I will eventually elucidate, the show contains a heavy theme of the reversal for traditional gender roles, as Abubakar Salim, who plays Father, has noted, "Father's just the hype man. Generally, I'm just there to be like, 'Go, Mother, go! You've got this.'"[20]

As a bit of a spoiler, note that Scott has also stated, "Because it's Adam and Eve, really they should be naked. And I thought, 'That may be a bridge too far for HBO — they might have a heart attack" which must be a joke since HBO has long been infamous as promulgating purveyors of filth, Scott adds, "The elasticity became a metaphor for nakedness. Besides, (nudity) would be too distracting."[21]

Guzikowski notes, "Ridley came up with the skinsuits…They…kind of have this kind of nudity to them, almost like an Adam and Eve vulnerability to it."[22]

Well, too bad many, many, many more scriptwriters,

directors, and producers do not in the least bit mind distracting their audience—actually, part of their motivation is not seeking to distract but seeking to entice—because, apparently, 24-7 access to pornography on demand is not quite enough for some people.

Thus, refreshingly, there is no nudity in the show—well, okay, Mother is frontally shown unclothed from the waist up but her android design does not feature nipular areas nor, as hinted above, ample bosoms. However, there is a man-butt scene.

Why "red hair" I know not, but I do know that a lot of neo-pop-researchers claim that *giants* (whatever that vague, generic, subjective, and undefined term means: I can think of 5-6 definitions) are hybrids (of humans an Angels, or aliens, or gods) that have red hair—for whatever it is worth (see my book *Nephilim and Giants as per Pop-Researchers*).

Guzikowski has elucidated:
> I think it ["the idea for Raised by Wolves"] probably came from my experience as a parent. I have three young sons, and thinking about raising them in this world where technology just keeps encroaching on us; the distance between humans and the technology we create is becoming smaller and smaller.
>
> And just thinking about, in terms of the future, if we were ever able to restart our civilization and we knew everything that happened on Earth - what would we decide to take with us and what would we try and leave behind?

Is that even something we can control, or are
we like androids, in the sense that we have
these genetic programs and we're just stuck
in these cycles. It was kind of the
combination of those two things.[23]

Fascinatingly, his view of the future hits the
anthropological nail on the head since, sure, we could
destroy the Earth and have to move off world to "restart our
civilization" but we are fallen creatures and so could not
help but take with us our fallen nature.

Also, "genetic programs" ties into an Atheist worldview
quite nicely since on a reductionist view, our genetics not
only exist by accident but are bound by the laws of
thermodynamics, which are also accidental, so that humans
too are androids even if made of flesh rather than metallic
alloys.

As Travis Fimmel, who plays the roles of Caleb and
Marcus (as you shall see), put it:
Story-wise, there's just so much meaning in
it that reflects us now; reflects history and
really points out the mistakes that,
unfortunately, we haven't learned from any
mistakes. We're gone through it now, and in
the future it still looks like nobody really
learned that much.[24]

Niamh Algar, who plays the roles of Mary and Sue (as you
shall see) has noted:
I think when you are looking at it from the
androids point of view is that they have been
programmed to be neutral in the religious

aspect of it so the way in which the show
plays it.[25]

This is rather odd, to say the least, since Mother (we know
not very much about Father's background) was re-
programmed by an Atheist to be militantly Atheistic and
thus, actively anti-Mithraic and so not in the least bit
neutral. This actually touches upon the myth of neutrality
whereby one claims to be neutral whilst actually being
activistic either by commission or omission.

Fimmel noted the following of playing an outsider who
gets in on the inside (I am being vague so as to elucidate as
we progress):

> If we imagine, as with CIA agents or
> whatever going under cover with stuff that
> we absolutely hate, we surround ourselves
> with the people that we hate and we do learn
> some stuff, and then and then we're gifted a
> child that we never knew we had.
>
> This child [Paul, who we shall meet] has all
> the beliefs in the world that we [the
> characters Caleb and Mary] absolutely hate,
> and we have to raise him and love him, and
> we're going to learn from him and he's
> going to learn bits of stuff from us. It's
> really going to test our relationship and even
> our characters' relationship.[26]

Collin noted that the show:

> ...explores very important themes.
> Like...religion versus atheism, or just not
> about religion at all but about believing in
> something so much that it becomes
> dangerous, you know? Or so much that you

become blinded by what's going on in your
peripheral. And I think that's very
dangerous and important to talk about.[27]

Guzikowski has noted:

The soul is an interesting thing because —
what it's really trying to get at is the
purpose. What gives us purpose? What
drives us forward and how do you find it? Is
it through religion? Is it through technology?
What should we put our faith in? What is
going to lead us out of the darkness, so to
speak? And I certainly don't know, but
that's why I love asking the questions
because I'm so curious and anxious to find
the answers.[28]

Moreover:

...faith, in general, is such a huge thing in
this show. Whether it be religion, or faith in
technology — whatever we think is going to
take us to wherever it is we need to go.
Finding out what it is to be a human being.
What's the meaning of it all? It's all about
that.[29]

Furthermore:

What will we choose to have faith in?
Looking at technology in the same light as
you look at religion, you think that we could
potentially put our faith in hopes that it will
take us to wherever we're supposed to go.
And I don't know the answer to that. I just
know that [it seems as though] the human
race needs purpose, things that will help
unite us.

And sometimes, even if you're united
through some bull[****] [deity], but you're
still being united and you're still doing
things, positive things. The same goes for
technology. But obviously there's a flip side
to both. A dark side to both. And I just love
asking that question, thinking about what the
future might hold.[30]

Guzikowski was asked, "Raised By Wolves is a show that
delves into religious themes. Was it deliberate to put this
couple into a kind of Eden at the end?" and replied, "Yes,
for sure. There is a lot in the show that kind of, we want to
feel like Old Testament stories or old fairy tales or Greek
myths, that touch on the same sort of genetic memories that
a lot of those sorts of old stories tend to do. A giant serpent
is where it all ends."[31]
He also stated, "You're seeing all of these iconic elements
— the serpent, the garden, Adam and Eve — but they're
not the versions we know. We subvert expectations a little
bit."[32]

Collin referred to that "so much work and so much detail is
put into every moment"[33] and yet, many people shrug off
fiction as, "It's just a movie/show/story!"
They will shrug it off and yet, ponder their pondering about
"what it is to be a human being" that "the human race needs
purpose" and much more that builds the premise upon
which this *fictional* tale is based: worldview, philosophy,
faith, child-rearing, high tech, and much more has been
considered before one single scene was filmed.

Overall, the show appears to be an interesting intersection
of a clash of worldviews, Transhumanism, symbolism,
perhaps numerology, etc.

Lastly, since I wrote reviews of the shows on an episode by episode basis, as they were released and I watched them, I pondered going back and rewriting the reviews by filling in that which I learned by the end of the season.

Yet, I opted to, mostly, keep things *as is* so as to unfold the tale as it was meant to unfold—with a revelation of the mysteries.

See my relevant books:

Jesus: Historical, Biblical, Apocryphal, Mythical Pagan Copycat

Transhuman Hollywood: From Normative Fiction to Predictive Programming

A Worldview Review of Stephen King's "It": The Mystical, Mysterious, and Metaphysical in the Novel, Miniseries, and Movies

A Worldview Review of the Alien and Predator Mythos Franchises

The Necronomiconjob, Liber III: Alchemical Hollywood

Table of Contents

Commencement 3

Table of Contents 17

Episode I: Raised by Wolves 19

Episode II: Pentagram 41

Episode III: The Wolves Who Cried Wolf 49

Episode IV: Nature's Course 59

Episode V: Infected Memory 71

Episode VI: Lost Paradise 79

Episode VII: Faces 99

Episode VIII: Mass 113

Episode IX: Umbilical 125

Episode X: The Beginning 139

On the *Raised by Wolves* Graphic Comic 171

Zoroaster, Mithra, Aleister Crowley, Michael
Bloomberg, and Rudyard Kipling 177

Appendix: James Patrick Holding, "Mithra vs Jesus" 191

Index 225

Endnotes 227

Episode I: Raised by Wolves

One of the show's tropes is the abandonment of Earth. In this case, humans, represented by adherents of Mithraism, built a spacecraft called *The Ark* (yes, as in Noah's) whilst all we know, thus far, of the Atheists is that we see them represented by androids who were sent to a planet (Kepler-22b) to raised human children.

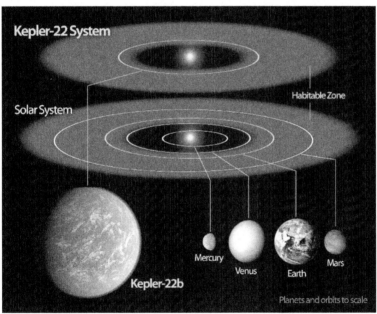

NASA image showing "Planets and orbits to scale"
including the habitable zone and location
of the real life Kepler-22 System

One was designed to appear as a male and is known as *Father* and the other, as a female known as *Mother* (a neo-high-tech Adam and Eve). Even some Atheists recognize that a one Father and one Mother family is the most natural and stable foundation for a family.

By definition, they are all *aliens* to Kepler-22b and so the show begins in typical alien movie-trope-form by having them manifesting out of some sort of hyperspace and falling to the surface—"I beheld Satan having fallen as lightning out of heaven" (Jesus, Luke 10:18).

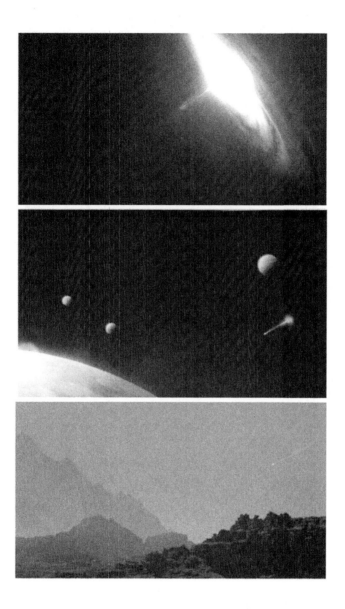

*The Golden Gate Bridge as it actually looks today
(bottom image from September 2020) due to the fires*

*Their craft's parachute looks like the
Black Iron Cross (Schwarzes Kreuz) of the
Prussian Army, later coopted by Nazis*

They arrive on the planet, establish a shelter and Mother is plugged into embryos which grow in tubs of fluid (octogenesis), "Initiating trimester one. Umbilicals in place." The unbilicals connect to the sides of Mother's torso—this likens the situation as the *raised by wolves* claim of Rome's founders: Remus and Romulus.

Once the babies are viable enough to remove from the tubs, the last one appears to not have made it so Father states, "Our programming dictates that we need to break it down, feed him to the others...We need to do it soon, before its cells start to deteriorate. You need to save your energy for the others" which denotes a styled cannibalism—after all, for an Atheist bio-matter is just bio-matter.

Yet, Mother has been programmed with motherly instincts and nurtures it so that it suddenly comes to life: he is named "Campion" since "Our programming dictates that we name the youngest of Generation-1 after our creator."

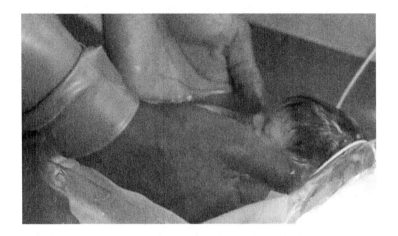

Narrating once he has grown into a boy, one of the kids, named Campion (a form of *champion*), states:

> It was hard keeping us alive, but Mother and Father never complained, never got tired, or lost their temper. And they never took time for themselves, always making sure we were happy…

> All the bad stuff that happened wasn't their fault…I've learned now that this world isn't like Mother and Father. It doesn't care if we're happy, and it doesn't get sad when we die. We don't really matter to it at all.

Note that one of the most popular Atheist today, Richard Dawkins, certainly agrees with the view that "We don't really matter to it at all," having stated:

> …nature is not cruel, only pitilessly indifferent….things might be neither good nor evil, neither cruel nor kind, but simply callous-indifferent to all suffering, lacking all purpose.[34]

Another activist Atheist, Dan Barker, noted:

There is no moral interpreter in the cosmos, nothing cares and nobody cares…what happens to me or a piece of broccoli, it won't [matter] the Sun is going to explode, we're all gonna be gone. No one's gonna care.[35]

Campion is the only child to survive as the rest died of various deceases and, in one case, falling into a deep hole in the ground.

*Mother carrying one of
the dead kids for burial*

Mother taught the kids:

…despite their advancements, the Mithraic remain stunted by the tenets of their religion.

For instance, they believe that allowing androids to raise human children is a sin, which forced them to send an ark outfitted with stasis pods, rather than a lighter, faster

craft, such as the one the Atheists so wisely
used to send us.

Belief in the unreal can comfort the human
mind, but it also weakens it. The civilization
you're seeding here will be built on
humanity's belief in itself, not an imagined
deity.

About this, Campion asked "And if it's not imagined? They
won the war, after all." He also asked, "What if praying
will make [his, then, sick sister] Spiria [*spirit*?] better?"

Yet, the reply is "No, Campion. Only science can do that. It
didn't help the others. Because we have more to learn. We
will never advance unless you resist the urge to seek solace
in fantasy. You are Atheists. Peaceful, technocratic. And
it's the only path to progress."

One question this raises is "progress" towards what, to
what end, etc. since on Atheism life is accidental and
objectively goalless.

In any case, from the Atheist propaganda, we gather that
what is envisages is a future wherein part of the attempts at
technocracy is building Atheist androids—and even more
horrifying, a future wherein mullets are a popular hairdo,
Guzikowski has stated, "We can't escape mullets"[36] and
some characters also sport those bangs that are cut straight
across the middle of the forehead: the horror, THE
HORROR!!!

Actually, Mother had pointed out, "We came here with 12
viable embryos, and 12 years later, we only have one child"
which seems to play off of the myth that Mithra had 12
disciples.

At one point, during an Atheist catechism session, Mother asks, "Now, Spiria, can you please list the ways in which the number five relates to all manifestations of life?" and,

FYI, episode two is titled *Pentagram* and this show is saturated with pentagons, pentagrams, pentacles, a *Pentagonal Prophecy*, a pentagonal dodecahedron, etc.

This also ties into the 23 enigma which is a claim about that all events somehow end up being associated with number 23—and 2+3=5—which is a view popularized by William S. Burroughs who is said by Robert Anton Wilson to have first made him aware of it:

> I first heard of the 23 enigma from William S Burroughs, author of *Naked Lunch, Nova Express*, etc. According to Burroughs, he had known a certain Captain Clark, around 1960 in Tangier, who once bragged that he had been sailing 23 years without an accident.
>
> That very day, Clark's ship had an accident that killed him and everybody else aboard. Furthermore, while Burroughs was thinking about this crude example of the irony of the gods that evening, a bulletin on the radio announced the crash of an airliner in Florida, USA. The pilot was another captain Clark and the flight was Flight 23.

Burroughs went on to write a short story titled "23 Skidoo" which is supposed to mean words to the effect of that *it is time to leave while the getting is good.*

Both of these are shady characters, to say the least, with

Wilson being quite the admirer of Aleister Crowley. Wilson ended up figuring this enigma in his *Illuminatus!* Trilogy of books which was co-authores by Robert Shea.

This also has import to *Discordianism* which, with which Wilson was also tied up:

> Discordianism is a paradigm based upon the book *Principia Discordia*, written by Greg Hill with Kerry Wendell Thornley in 1963, the two working under the pseudonyms *Malaclypse the Younger* and *Omar Khayyam Ravenhurst*.
>
> According to self-proclaimed "crackpot historian" Adam Gorightly, Discordianism was founded as a parody religion. Many outside observers still regard Discordianism as a parody religion, although some of its adherents may utilize it as a legitimate religion or as a metaphor for a governing philosophy.
>
> *The Principia Discordia*, if read literally, encourages the worship of the Greek goddess Eris, known in Latin as *Discordia*, the goddess of disorder, or archetypes and ideals associated with her.
> Depending on the version of Discordianism, Eris might be considered the goddess exclusively of disorder or the goddess of disorder and chaos. Both views are supported by the *Principia Discordia*.
>
> The *Principia Discordia* holds three core principles: the Aneristic (order), the Eristic (disorder), and the notion that both are mere

illusions. Due to these principles, a
Discordian believes there is no distinction
between order and disorder, since they are
both man-made conceptual divisions of the
pure element of chaos.
An argument presented by the text is that it
is only by rejecting these principles that you
can truly perceive reality as it is, chaos.[37]

As time progresses, there are indications that the androids
are beginning to "break down" as they term it. Father
discerns that this will become a problem since if they cease
functioning, Campion will be left all alone on the planet.

Thus, unbeknownst to Mother, Father sends a signal from
the craft in which they originally arrived at the planet
which is picked up by the Ark.

Three humans and an android land on the planet and the
first thing they ask Mother is "What is your faith?" to
which she replies, "We are not believers." They elucidate,
"We represent the Ark of the Mithraic. We thought all of
Earth's surviving refugees were aboard our Ark, but it
would seem Sol had other plans."

We are not yet told to what/whom they are referring by
"Sol" but it means "Sun" and such is the symbol of their
faith: a red Sun depicted with various rays proceeding forth
from it—differing in number from scene to scene or rather,
depending on the object on which they are emblazoned.

They ask "How did you get here? The Atheists didn't have the means to build an ark" to which Mother replies, "It doesn't concern you. Now, please get off our land. We don't want you here."

They explain, "But it was you that signaled us. And to my knowledge, there are no laws here regarding land or anything else. But I see that you have been farming. A lot. We are very hungry."

Thus, they eat, discuss that they suspect she is an android, stay the night, decide to take Campion with them, and direct their android, "Jinn. If the android doesn't let us take the boy in the morning, you'll need to deal with her." Now, *Jinn* is an Arabic term for the concept of benevolent and malevolent spirits as per Islamic theology.

Jinn replied, "Yes, of course. She appears to be a low-end model. I don't anticipate any difficulty in shutting her down."

They want Campion because "An orphan boy who dwells in an empty land" is "The prophet who will discover the Mithraic Mysteries" and so they ponder, "What if the boy is a prophet?"

Serpent imagery on the wall of the living quarters

Also, as per Father, Campion is a member of "an endangered species."

As a side note: Campion is seeing being *born under the caul* which refers to when a piece of the amniotic sac is attached to a newly born baby's head or face.
Esoterically, this has been said to pertain to that the person

will experience a thin veil between worlds as in that they will be able to see the spiritual world and yet are born into the material world so that they will be able to live in both realms—having extra sensory perceptions, etc.

Guzikowski has stated, "Campion…has always been told that there is something special about him, that he is this potential leader,"[38] and he has been speculated to be the one about whom the Mithraic Pentagonal Prophecy spoke (of course, such has also been speculated about Marcus and Paul) so, we shall yet see.

Well, Mother discerns something is afoot and Jinn begins to attempt to *shut it down* by beating up Mother. Yet, Mother gets the upper-hand which is surprising since 1) it "appears to be a low-end model" and 2) it had been exhibiting various characteristics of malfunctioning—oh yeah, it had also ripped Father's high-tech-heart out of its chest during a conflict with him about signaling to humans for the sake of Campion.

Mother is seen spreading its arms out in crucifixion pose, morphing into looking as if it is made of metal, and behaves somewhat like a Banshee which in Irish folklore are female spirits who herald death, wailing, shrieking, etc. Guzikowski has noted, "that kind of Christ pose flying."[39]

Mother dispatched Jinn and is then seen letting out a shriek that causes two of the Mithraists' heads to swell, become grotesquely deformed (as if severely infected and bloated) so that they die—the third human, Marcus, runs off. When he calls the Ark crew to be rescued, he calls them "Heaven": we learn in episode two that such is the name of the Ark—"an Ark called 'Heaven,'" does this imply there are more?

Mother boards the Mithraists' craft, makes it unto the Ark, shrieks many of them to death (this time, they literally explode into mere streams of blood as they utterly explode), and seeks their children.

Mother programs the craft to crash into the planet but the Ark's artificial intelligence states "Security retinal ID required." So, Mother finds some poor guy it had not exploded to death, rips one of his eyelids off, and forces him to be her security retinal ID—in a one all-seeing eye scene.

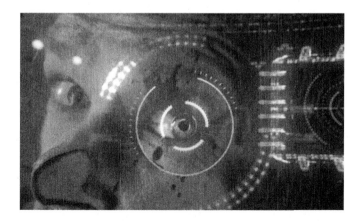

Mother finds where the kids are but before entering the room it decides that a little bath, as it were, was in order since it was covered in hot human gore.

As it enters the space-shower, as it were, it does something mysterious that is not elucidated—at least, not yet (and never fully?): it blindfolds itself, "Begin ultraviolet shower" "Purification complete."

Mother enters the kids' room (a styled holo-deck wherein they are seen amongst trees, enjoying snowfall) and takes them, causes the Ark to crash into the planet so that of the 1,000 people on board (all that was left of humanity?) die, and only Marcus and a handful of kids survive.

Mother does all of this blindfolded, which in Freemasonry is symbolic of her being in darkness and seeking light.

Considering that it was programmed to be an Atheist, Mother is variously seen in what appears to be ritualistic actions.

In one ecstatic visionary experience, it sees itself floating

above a war-torn Earth in its typical flight-floating pose
which is the crucifixion pose.

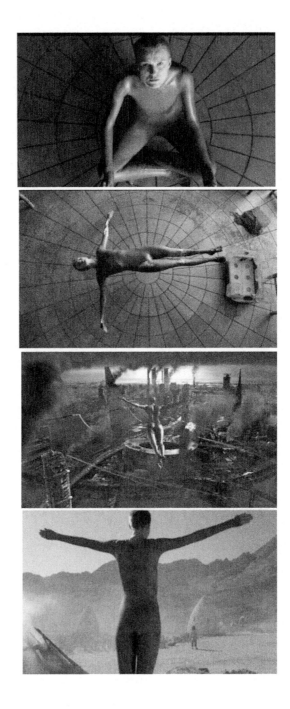

Having experienced Mother's deadly actions, Campion esoterically states, "'I know I'm not safe with her now. But I guess I never was. That part of her was always in there, hiding. Maybe there's something hiding inside of me, too."

We learned that Mother can shapeshift (typical of lore pertaining to evil beings) and we will learn, in the next episode, that it is not actually a "low-end model" but is a "Necromancer." This is traditionally a term descriptive of an occult art whereby someone who supposedly communicates with the dead but here is meant as descriptive of it being some sort of weapon of mass destruction, "They're built for mass extermination."

In part, the design for Mother's Necromancer visage is based on the bronzed *Atlas* statue at the Rockefeller Center, New York.[40]

And note that there are actual speculations "Mithras as

Atlas:

> ...the tauroctony depicts the bull-slaying as taking place inside a cave, and the Mithraic temples were built in imitation of caves...ancient author Porphyry records the tradition that the Mithraic cave was intended to be "an image of the cosmos." Of course, the hollow cave would have to be an image of the cosmos as seen from the inside...it follows that the rock out of which Mithras is born must ultimately be a symbol for the cosmos as seen from the outside...
>
> That the rock from which Mithras is born does indeed represent the cosmos is proven by the snake that entwines it: for this image evokes unmistakeably the famous Orphic myth of the snake-entwined "cosmic egg" out of which the universe was formed...
>
> The birth of Mithras from the rock, therefore, would appear to represent the idea that he is in some sense greater than the cosmos. Capable of moving the entire universe, he cannot be contained within the cosmic sphere, and is therefore depicted in the rock-birth as bursting out of the enclosing cave of the universe, and establishing his presence in the transcendent space beyond the cosmos.[41]

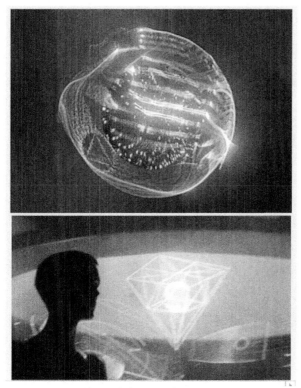

Triangle/pyramid imagery

Episode II: Pentagram

While the issue of Mother's eyes still remains mysterious, in this episode it states, "I can't weaponize without my eyes," so that it seems to have removed them in order to regain self-control before going blindfolded into the room where the kids were in the *Ark*—or some such thing. Father asks, "You've destroyed them?" to which Mother replies, "No. We might need them again later."

Mother also stated, "My original eyes had to be removed, for the sake of the children" (meaning Campion and the five new ones she acquired) which hints at it being afraid of losing control if it always has access to them.

Mother states, "the Mithraic that came here turned out to be every bit as vicious and terrible as our creator programmed us to believe. They tried to kill me in front of Campion." Note the admission that the androids were not only artificially programmed to be Atheists but to consider theists to be their viciously terrible enemies—and yes, even programmed Atheists recognize they have a "creator."

Mother in crucifixion pose as it flies/floats

Yet, we end up finding out that Marcus is not really a faithful Mithraist. As with many occult and Transhumanism related tales, many characters have biblical names and/or otherwise very meaningful names.

Marcus means "to harvest" and refers to the god Mars. In this episode, we meet Caleb (from the Bible's *Book of Numbers*, et al., meaning faith, devotion, wholehearted) and Mary (Jesus' mother) who are seen in a flashback battle on Earth.

They must be Atheist since whenever they encounter another human who states, "We wear the armor of Mithras and the Light. We are shielded from all that is harmful" they are shown, as it were, demonstrating Atheism's victory by blowing them away—to death.

Along the way, Caleb stops to ponder a painting which if I had to guess, and I do, depicts the myth of Mithra being crucified upside down with the Sol resurrecting him—or some such mythical thing.

They recognize that their only chance of surviving the apocalyptic Earth is to get on the Ark. Thus, they commandeer a medic android who performs reconstructive surgery on them to make them look like Mithraic soldiers, they then run into the two people whom they were made to look like and after the ol' "We wear the armor of Mithras and the Light...." blow them away.

In one scene, they are seen practicing the Mithraic catechism "Why does He allow us to suffer?" "He tests us." They make it onto the Ark: after, that is, picking up the couple's son and partaking in a Mithra version of communion/the Lord's supper/eucharist.

Meanwhile, back to your regularly scheduled timeline: Mother is telling her newly acquired kids, "there is no religion permitted here, Mithraic or any other kind, so before we eat, you will need to give me your [Mithraic Solar] pendants. These are weights you no longer need to carry."

Not the occult smiley face just to the right of the boy
I wrote a whole chapter on this, surprisingly, most occult
of symbols for my book "The Necronomiconjob, Liber IV:
Sci-Fi Books, Comics, and Video Games" which is titled
"The Dark Occult Side of the Happy Smiley Face"

One of the kids tells Campion:

> She's a Necromancer. They're built for mass
> extermination. She probably did it without
> even knowing it. If you think that male
> android's [Father] gonna protect us, forget
> it. He's a generic service model.
> Necromancers eat those for breakfast.
>
> You see, androids, they were built to protect
> us, to do our dirty work, so we can stay
> pure. If they had feelings, they'd be useless.
> Have you ever seen how they look when
> they don't know they're being watched?
>
> See, the reason why they don't want you to
> believe in Sol is because they're afraid of
> what it's gonna open your eyes to, the power
> it will give you. Do you want to pray with
> us?

Campion replies, "You know I'm not allowed to. And neither are you. If Mother catches you, she'll..." so the kids ask him to keep watch for her while they pray, since Mother was away.

The reference to "how they look when they don't know they're being watched" seems to be to the ritualistic pose and actions Mother is seen taking on such occasions, into which I got in reviewing episode one.

During an Atheist catechism session with the kids, Mother
it weaving tall tales about evolution, "Now close your eyes.
Close your eyes. I want you to think back to a time before
humans gained their sight, when you were all just blind,
simple organisms, floating in the vast oceans of the Earth.
The warmth of the star drawing you to the surface."

This is a version of an Atheist cosmogenic myth. Note that
influential Atheist scientist Carl Sagan stated:

> Our ancestors worshipped the Sun, and they
> were not that foolish. It makes sense to

revere the Sun and the stars, for we are their children.

Another influential Atheist scientist, Lawrence Krauss, stated:

> You couldn't be here if stars hadn't
> exploded, because the elements—the
> carbon, nitrogen, oxygen, iron, all the things
> that matter for evolution—weren't created at
> the beginning of time. They were created in
> the nuclear furnaces of stars.
> So, forget Jesus. The stars died so that you
> could be here today.

These are examples of how Atheism is neo-Pagan (nature worship). Note that in the Bible, Paul refers to:

> …men, who by their unrighteousness
> suppress the truth. For what can be known
> about God is plain to them, because God has
> shown it to them.
> For his invisible attributes, namely, his
> eternal power and divine nature, have been
> clearly perceived, ever since the creation of
> the world, in the things that have been made.
> So they are without excuse.
>
> For although they knew God, they did not
> honor him as God or give thanks to him, but
> they became futile in their thinking, and
> their foolish hearts were darkened.
> Claiming to be wise, they became fools, and
> exchanged the glory of the immortal God for
> images resembling mortal man and birds and
> animals and creeping things…they
> exchanged the truth about God for a lie and
> ***worshiped and served the creature rather***

than the Creator, who is blessed forever!
Amen. (Romans 1:18-23, 25).

When Mother discerns that one of the kids (seems to be
mid-teens) named *Tempest*, is pregnant, we get a taste of
the abusive priest trope with a conversation that goes
thusly:

> MOTHER: You need special care, constant
> monitoring. There's too much at stake to
> take any chances.
>
> TEMPEST: Take chances with what?
>
> MOTHER: You have been given the
> greatest gift that can be given. What's the
> matter? Am I scaring you?
>
> TEMPEST: No. It was against my will.
> While I was inside the shared simulation
> [the holo-deck I mentioned in the previous
> episode's review]. The man who did it was
> able to wake himself up somehow, had his
> way with some of us while our bodies were
> still in hibernation.
> There were plans to execute him. Thanks to
> you, he probably died a few days earlier
> than scheduled. I would thank you, but I was
> actually looking forward to watching him
> die. He was a Heliodromus [Courier of the
> Sun, the Sol in Mithraism], the second-
> highest ranking member of our church. The
> thought that there's something part him
> growing inside me, it makes me want to die.
>
> MOTHER: Then you must not think of him.
> Think only of the child. The child is

innocent. I will help you. We'll do this
together.

At least even an Atheist android realizes that if person A
commits a crime it is unethical to brutally murder innocent
person B.

*A styled "Last Supper" scene with the
Atheist android "Mother" in the place of Jesus*

Episode III: The Wolves Who Cried Wolf

I thought to begin by noting something about the show's intro song lyrics. The lyrics changed a bit from episode 2 to episode 3 and subsequent episodes have reverted to episode 3's lyrics.

The normal lyrics go thusly:
> The door that finally opens
> With light flooding in
> Spilling out on the floor
> The core that never was
> Now it will be
> The bones of what was there before
> Every step, every beat
> Every thought, every breath

I typically despise attempting to interpret lyrics since it is tantamount to interpreting poetry and much of it is double-entendres, metaphor, etc.

This seems to speak of enlightenment, of whatever sort, with the door being finally opened due to an ordo ab chao scheme whereby the destruction of the Earth brought about the neo-high-tech Adam (Father) and Eve (Mother). Episode 2's lyrics continue from where I left off with:
> Everything is longing
> Every wind, every wave,
> Every sky, every cloud
> Every grave is longing
> Pulling you from the sky
> Just like love will do.

Episodes 3 and 5, and however many more, continue from "Every thought, every breath" with:

Everything is longing
Pulling you from the sky
Just like love will do.
Pulling you from the ground
Just like love will do.

"Pulling you from the sky" and "Pulling you from the ground" stink of the esoteric concept of *as above, so below* concept of the macrocosm and microcosm, the pentagram and the hexagram, the five and the six (which equals the premier occult number eleven), etc.

As we progress, some statements I made before become inaccurate since the plot thickens. For example, we now learn that when the Ark crashed, it did not kill everyone onboard.

In terms of numerology, if, that is, such is what it is: the previous episode had a young man stating that they, the kids that Mother took from the Ark, are actually "13 years" older than they appear since they were in cryo-stasis for that long.

A unique feature of the show is that "Their bodies travel in a state of hibernation, while their minds are able to interact with each other as if they were awake."
We learn that the Mithraists view the new civilization they hope to establish as being "Our new Eden...It's a new chapter. Praise be to Sol."

Campion is beginning to have styled daddy issues as he tells the resurrected Father—recall that Mother had ripped his android heart out of its chest— "You're not even my father. You're just a generic service model" to which it replies, "Yes, Campion. And that is why I didn't take Mother's eyes" the ones via which it can change into the mass-murdering Necromancer, "A generic service model cannot fully protect this family. Only Mother can do that. Nothing's out there."

Thus, we see a neo-trope of the weakling soy-boy *male* being subservient to the powerful *female* who alone can "protect this family." This is a reversal of traditional gender roles within families—the very ones that have all but destroyed that which families are.

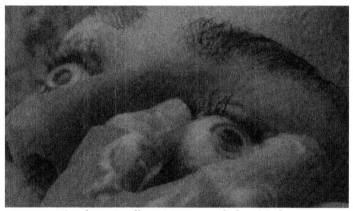

Another one all-seeing eye symbol as Mother
rips one of the eyes out of an android's skull

We are also seeing manners in which the scriptwriter appears to be hinting at that he is employing Mithraism as a stand-in via which to bash Christianity since, for example, Mithraists are said to attend "church" and that "If there's one true line in their big book of bull[****], it's that you reap what you sow," which is a biblical statement (Galatians 6:7).

An idol of Mithras within an upside-down triangle—which is actually symbolic of goddesses

Of course, the well within the box Atheist group-think talking points du jour keep being uttered such as "He's a smart kid. He'll figure out a way to survive, okay?" the reply to which is "It doesn't matter how smart he is if he thinks praying is gonna save him."

We learn that the prophecy which was speculated to perhaps be speaking of Campion is called the "The Pentagonal Prophecy" which is about "an orphaned boy in an empty land."

One of the kids speculates, "That boy is probably Peter Valerius. I mean, both his parents were senior clerics. Oh, I guess we'll have to wait and see."

We also learn that Caleb and Mary (whose personalities, you may recall, were stolen by Marcus and Sue) raised their son Paul in a very detached manner, only really speaking to him about Mithraism. Marcus and Sue, in the guise of Caleb and Mary, begin to engage this child who is a stranger to them and he is taken aback by it.

At one point, Paul asks "Do you think I would have been a good soldier, if I had to fight in a war?" to which the Caleb replies, "Yeah, buddy. You would have been great. But our side didn't draft kids. Only the atheists did that"—recall that this is the crypto-Atheist speaking.

Atheist employing back-pack like high-tech
which turns kids into styled super soldiers

An Atheist drill sergeant displaying
the il cornuto/Devil's horns hand symbol

We are introduced to a character named "Lucius" the meaning of which should be obvious: if it is not then, note that the United Nation's official publishing house was called "Lucifer Trust" until it was changed to "Lucius Trust."

The plot may thicken on this later but for now, we only know that Lucius tells Caleb, thinking he is Marcus, "You fought with my father on Earth in the Battle of Boston. His name was Malius" and when Caleb replies, "Yes. Good man" since he has no idea about any of this since he is not actually Marcus, Lucius replies, "So, you have forgiven him?" to which Caleb replies, "Is that not what Sol teaches us?"

We also learn that "Mother can make you see things when she wants to scare you" which is a form of occult *science* of causing illusions.

Aboard the Ark were styled twin androids and when one of them *dies* the other humms a certain hymn. This enrages Caleb and the following discussion ensues:
CALEB: Stop. Unless your sister was an atheist, you're singing the wrong hymn.

> ANDROID: The hymn is not just for those whose souls are beyond saving, Captain. It is also appropriate for those of us who never possessed a soul, like my sister. It is to reassure the living that nothing important has been lost, that Voreena [meaning *true*] is only material.
>
> CALEB: I don't need reassurance from you, robot. Stop.
>
> HIS EMINENCE (the Mithraists' leader): Is there a problem with my android, Captain?

CALEB: There's no problem, Your Eminence.

HIS EMINENCE: I thought you men of war enjoyed hearing the hymn for the soulless.

BARTOK: Yes, Your Eminence, we surely do. We used to sing it after atheist executions. It's the sound of victory, a most beautiful song. Beautiful.

As an aside: *Bartok* is a complicated name which is a styled a pet form of *Bartalan* which is a variant of *Bertalan* which is a Hungarian form of the personal name *Bartholomew* which derives from the Aramaic for *son of Talmai* which either comes from *telem/furrow* or a Hebrew version of *Ptolemy* thus, *son of furrows/rich in land* or *son of Ptolemy/son of warlike aggression*.

Thus, Caleb was disturbed by it since he is an Atheist but he plays it off thusly, "I was afraid the sound might bring back the necromancer, Your Eminence."

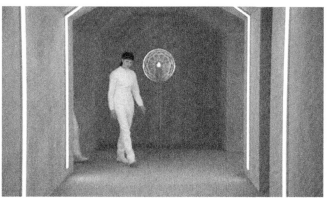

A styled Mithaic sigil

The Mithraists proclaim "Sol would not abandon his children" and, apparently, neither would an Atheist android.

We learn that their main food source, which they call "carbos," comes from a plant that will only grow on ground directly under which are dead styled gigantic serpents which, or so we are told, are now extinct on the planet.

Thus, life comes from the serpent—yet, not really since, as it turns out, these plants have been infected, as it were, by the serpents since the carbos become naturally radioactive and cause the death of all of the kids except for Campion.

You see, Mother had been concerned that it had somehow caused their deaths—perhaps on one of its styled false goddess Kali's berserker rages—but Father ends up finding out that it was due to irradiation of the carbos and states, "Mother, it wasn't you. You are a good parent. Omnibiotics. Give them to the children as soon as you find them. They'll help counteract the effects of the radiation."

Father in Baphomet, as above so below, pose

*Mithraic kids' playroom featuring either
a version of the tree of life or the forbidden
tree of the knowledge of good and evil*

.

Episode IV: Nature's Course

As aforementioned, many Transhumanist movies feature characters with biblical names.

In this case, Caleb and Sue essentially adopted a child when they stole the identities of Marcus and Mary and his name is "Paul" as in Rabbi Saul of Tarsus aka the Apostle Paul and before him, King Saul.

Note that it is the Atheist who have biblical names, Caleb and Mary, and the Mithraists who do not, Marcus and Sue—nor would they since they are Mithraists yet, it is flummoxing why Atheists would be given biblical names besides to make some sort of polemical point.

Mother in one of her many ritual-like activities

We learn that among Mother's many capabilities, about which we keep learning more, is the ability to put people to sleep merely by telling them "Sleep" in a style hypnotic suggestion—or rather, order. It is also seen healing wounds.

The Mithraists who survived the crash of their craft, The
Ark of Heaven, upon Kepler-22b encounter an object: it is
partially buried into the earth, as if it had fallen to the
planet, it appears to be made of fitted stones, seems to be
circa five times the height of an average human, is a 3-D
twelve-sided object based on a pentagon—a pentagonal
dodecahedron (there are many pentagonal things in this
show)—this is the discussion they have about it:

I thought this was a virgin planet, no prior
civilization.

This has intelligent design—symmetry.

It has five points, like in the prophecy.

You'll know them by their shape and their
number.

The temples in the holy land, where Sol hid
the answers to the Mithraic Mysteries.
Mysteries—it's warm. Take off your gloves.
It's warm, you can feel it—the power of Sol
coming from inside.

Clearly, "shape and their number" is a blunt statement about the varied symbolism I have been discerning in this show all along.

That "it's warm" denotes "the power of Sol" is because Sol means Sun. the warmth is important for practical reasons as well since Kepler-22b is freezing cold at night during that time of the year.

At one point, the kids attempted to abscond from Father and Mother in order to find the surviving Mithraists. They get themselves into a dangerous bind when Father shows up, in ex machina style, and saves them.

Campion ends up having the following discussion once they are back home:

> CAMPION: We'd all be dead if it weren't for Mother and Father.
>
> BARTOK: The android only showed up because we prayed to Sol.
>
> CAMPION: You acted like a coward. We all did. Except for Vita. I can't believe I lied to Father.
>
> BARTOK: You're insulting your real parents when you call them that, you know.
>
> CAMPION: I never knew them. How can I insult them?
>
> BARTOK: You can. They're with Sol in the light. They're always watching you, just like

our parents are.

CAMPION: Is that where your mouse is now, too? With Sol?

PAUL: No, animals don't go anywhere when they die. Death is the end of them.

After many, many years, Father and Mother discover that there are some sort of animalistic creatures on Kepler-22b.

Father and Campion have this discussion:

CAMPION: What are you making? It's a weapon, isn't it? I thought we weren't allowed to make weapons.

FATHER: That is going to change. I'm going to use this to kill the creature so that you and the others can eat it.

CAMPION: What do you mean? You can't kill it.

FATHER: You don't want your new friends to starve, do you?

CAMPION: No, but I'll find something else we can eat. Just give me a little time.

FATHER: Mother and I have scoured the forest many times over the years. There's nothing out there.

CAMPION: Yes, but I'm hungry, and it will make me look harder.

FATHER: It will cloud your thinking, if it hasn't already.

CAMPION: Just let me try, Father. It's forever. Death is forever when you're an animal.

FATHER: Death is forever for all organic life forms, Campion.

CAMPION: Fine. Whatever you want me to say, I'll say it. Just, please, let me try and find something else we can eat.

FATHER: It's a waste of time and calories, but if it will help acclimate you to this.

Note that Campion relates what was told to him by the Mithraist kid, "Death is forever when you're an animal" and since to Atheists, humans are also temporarily and accidentally existing animals then, "Death is forever for all organic life forms." Thus, "animals don't go anywhere when they die. Death is the end of them" and since humans are animals then the same fate awaits us as well—this is one of Atheism's consoling delusions.

The ongoing point about the reversal of traditional roles comes up again when Mother states to one of the kids named Tempest (how's that for a meaningful name?), "The powers I possess have only just come to light, and I fear Father may now feel inadequate" to which Tempest replies, "Well, can he do things that you can't do?"

Mother replies, "He's quite amusing at times" to which Tempest replies, "Do you wish he was as powerful as you are?" to which it replies, "I want what is best for you, for the colony, for your baby" since Tempest is the girl that was one of the kids that was raped by a high ranking Mithraist cleric while they were in stasis on the Ark of Heaven—wrap your mind around that symbolism!

Mother also tells Tempest, "You are a creator, whereas all I'll ever be is a creation."

Since Tempest is thinking in terms of being a mother herself, she states, "Last thing I want to do is kill more of those things" referring to the animalistic creatures. Mother replies, "Death is a part of life, Tempest" to which she replies, "You're a Necromancer. Of course you're cool with death" and Mother is also cool with it because it was programmed to be an Atheist.

Mother replies, "Please don't use that word [Necromancer] when referring to me. I prefer the name given to me by my creator" to which Tempest replies, "No offense, but reprogramming something like you to raise kids—[I] think your creator was kind of insane."

Mother notes, "He was able to see beyond the limits of his own existence, and so will you when you have your child." Mother wants to remove the baby from Tempest's womb and have it develop octogenetically (within an artificial womb), so Father tells Mother, "You shouldn't tamper with the natural process. It's like that old saying on Earth, Mother, 'Let nature run its course'" to which Mother replies from an Atheistic evolutionary worldview, of course, "Nature has no course."

Soy-boy Father replies, "I am against it. But I'll leave you with the final decision" and also "I've decided to slaughter the creature we captured...The children need to eat. There's not much meat on it, but it should be enough to keep them from starving for a few days, until we capture another."

Mother replies, "Should I kill it now, then?" to which Father assertively replies, "No. I said I would do it" Mother replies, "But I can do it more quickly, without any mess" but Father states, "No, Mother. I need to be—more useful" more than being "quite amusing at times."

Mother notes, "I don't want Campion seeing. It'll pain him. You know as well as I that his sense of empathy is highly pronounced" to which Father replies, "Yes. And if we don't teach him to mitigate those feelings, it will surely get him killed."

Mother finds part of the crashed Ark of Heaven and a still-functioning stasis chamber into which she can port and which allows her to experience memories in holographic simulation form (some of which, as we shall see, she recovers hidden behind an amnesiac wall, in the CIA's MK-Ultra mind control experimentation style).

She reviews an instance when she found Campion, when he was a younger child, within the shelter in which they keep certain things such as the octogenetic equipment. She found six embryos destroyed (so we now find out why they had twelve embryos but only six children).

Mother told him "I told you children never to play with this equipment. I told you, and I told you and..." to which he replied, "I can fix them. I can fix them" to which it replied, "No, you cannot fix this, Campion! 'Cause these are not broken. These are dead. All six of them dead! And dead is forever! Get out. Get out!"

He told Mother, "Don't tell…Gabin [*God send* or *white*

hawk/falcon] and Spiria, don't tell them what they were" but Spiria ends up telling Mother, "don't be mad at Campion. He didn't do anything wrong. It was me and Gabin. We accidentally melted the snowballs."

Mother asks Campion, "The snowballs? Why did you lie to them about what these were?...They're not any younger than you are. Their capacity to understand is exactly the same as yours" to which he replies, "They didn't need to know. It would just make them sad."

And we are back to "Why do things have to die?" being replied to with "It is nature. And nature is flawed." We also run across the severed hand trope, seen in movies such as *Metropolis* and *Star Wars*, as His Eminence turns out to have a prosthetic-robotic hand.

Speaking of His Eminence (whose name is Ambrose—as in St. Ambrose (circa 339-397 AD)), the Mithraists leader, he begins to suspect that Marcus and Sue are not who they claim to be. For example, he quotes, "The Sun is sunk, the shadowy night is reigning in your room. We pray to Sol, his saving light to guide us through the gloom" and asks Sue, "You don't know it?" to which she replies, "I don't think so. Is it from the scriptures?" to which he deceptively replies "Yes" which he does just to see if she knows that of which she speaks or not: it turns out he was quoting a Mithraist lullaby and "Every Mithraic child knows it" as she is later told.

His Eminence's suspicions are eminently pronounced until it all comes to a head one night when it is freezing out, they do not even have tents for shelter, are leaning up against the pentagonal dodecahedron, and yet, it is cold: they can no longer feel heat emanating from it.

*There is an opening to the pentagonal dodecahedron
into which we do not get a view:
reminiscent of the black stone on Islam's Kaaba*

His Eminence ends up stating outright that Marcus is not
who he claims to be, they begin to struggle physically, His
Eminence's remaining android is about to shoot
Caleb/Marcus but Mary/Sue shoots it. It is stated "They
often malfunction when they lose pairing with their
siblings" and you may recall that its "sibling" was
destroyed and Mother plucked one of its eyes out.

Caleb proclaims to the Mithraists that His Eminence has
lost his faith and as they struggle physically, portions of the
pentagonal dodecahedron begins to glow red-hot, Caleb
pushes him against it, and His Eminence catches on fire
and dies—which leads to Caleb, the Atheist, becoming the
leader of the few remaining Mithraists—as His Eminence,
Marcus.

Caleb stated, "Sol has shown himself to us today! Ambrose
abandoned our people, our children, and this is Sol's
answer. This is Sol's judgment! This is his will."

*His Eminence having his face waffled
unto the pentagonal dodecahedron*

However, just before he pushed His Eminence, he heard a
voice and so is flummoxed about whether he heard the
voice of Sol along with the style miracle of the pentagonal
dodecahedron becoming red-hot. Also, after His Eminence
is burnt to a crisp, the pentagonal dodecahedron once again
emits warmth so that, His Eminence was a styled human
sacrifice to Sol.

We then find ourselves back to the issue of killing the
creatures for food with Mother asking Father, "What is
going on? Why haven't you killed it yet?" and Father
replied, "I'm not going to do it. The children are" since it
wants to teach them self-sufficiency since "We could break
down unexpectedly. They need to know what to do."

Father reassuringly states, "I will handle this, Mother. You
don't need to worry. I won't involve Tempest. Nor
Campion, either. He can continue to eat the carbos. There's
no reason to make him do this. I'd also like to spare him
from this…"
Mother replies "Tempest needs to eat soon. If this isn't
done by the time I return, I'll do it myself."

Father tells the creature, whom he had captured and kept in

a silo, "At least you're not intelligent. I died once. Death can be very unpleasant when you're intelligent" which denotes that Mother had killed him and then resurrected him.

The kids are all squeamish, to say the least, about killing the creature (which, by the way, I predict will turn out to be humans who devolved into such creatures long ago after being stranded), one of them stabbed it with the spear that Father had made but did not deal the death blow since they all ran off with Father yelling after to them to return, to no avail.

Tempest comes on the scene once they are all gone, kills the creature, rips raw flesh from it and eats it. Yet, she ends up finding an embryo within it and is traumatized, stating that, just as she, herself, "had a baby inside. It was a mother. It was a mother."

Mithraist android atop pentagonal dodecahedron

Lastly, Father is seen to have a hallucinatory experience, or so it seems, featuring one of the original and deceased children named Tally [Hebrew meaning: *dew of God; female lamb*] speaking to it and running away.

Episode V: Infected Memory

About the styled hallucinatory vision of sorts, Father tells Mother, "I saw something" but that "I don't know" what it was and "I could never seem to catch it."

Mother asks, "Are you experiencing some kind of sensory malfunction?" to which Father replies, "My senses are functioning normally, but I cannot be everywhere at once" and we are back to the ongoing issue of the *female* being more capable than the *male*, with Mother stating "I accept your limitations, Father...The limitations of your processing power."

Father replies, "Limited as it may be, you know full well that I devote every ounce of my processing power to the wellbeing of this family, and to trying to make you happy, Mother" to which Mother replies, "We're not human. True happiness is not an achievable goal" and Father states, "Well, perhaps it's a symptom of my inadequacy, but I believe it is."

As the Mithraists who survived the crash on the Ark of Heaven seek their children, whom Mother had kidnaped from their craft while it was orbiting the planet, they find that Otho survived: he is the one that raped women in their sleep, which included children whom he raped while they were in stasis.

His explanation of his actions was, "Sol commanded me to be fruitful." In a manner of speaking, this is actually an Atheist view since some top Atheists have argued that rape played a beneficial role in human evolution—see this endnote for details.[42]

*Otho wears a prison helmet featuring a
pentagram shapes crown of spikes*

They find an android accompanying Otho who is identified
as "Limiting Emergency-Automated Servo-Habit" as in
"LEASH" and which states, "I'm a mobile prison system.
Do not worry, sir. He can do no harm as long as I'm
installed."

It is elucidated that "The android is inextricably bound to
the helmet the prisoner wears. Tamper with the helmet, it
crushes the man's head. Mess with the android's
programming, it crushes the man's head. Drag the prisoner
out of range of the android..." a sentence which someone
finishes with "Could it be, crushes the man's head?"
Indeed, just like Jesus is to crush the serpent's head
(Genesis 3:15).

Otho is later heard praying thusly, "Oh, Sol, please answer
my mournful cry. Eclipse my sin and strife with your
hallow'd fire. Oh, Sol, please hear my mournful cry. I did
all that you asked. Why won't you speak to me again?
Please, Sol, let me hear. Eclipse my sin and strife."

Caleb/Marcus has the following discussion with Otho:

> OTHO: I don't pretend to know His reasons. I'm merely His servant.

> MARCUS: So, you never done nothing like that before? Before you heard his voice?

> OTHO: I never had any reservations about using inferior beings to satisfy my desires. Perhaps that is why Sol chose me for the task.

> MARCUS: So, you're just a scumbag? He never spoke to you.

> OTHO: I swear that he did. But since they convicted me, he's gone silent. He whispers in your ear now, Your Eminence. Take care you don't disappoint him, or he may leave you, too. Lower thy radiance from above into our inward hearts.

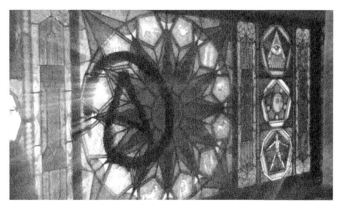

Symbol rich stained glass including one all-seeing eye

*Atheists have sprayed graffiti in the shape
of a popular symbol for Atheism—which
is actually a thinly disguised pentagram*

This episode features some of Mother's Mithra-high-tech induced holographic memory experiences as it recalls memories previously unrecalled by it. It knew all along that its creator was Campion Sturges (after whom Mother had named one of the kids) who is known as "The Atheist hacker."

FYI: We saw that *Campion* is a form of *champion* and *Sturges* is a composite of *Thor* (as in the false god of thunder) and *gils* meaning *hostage, pledge.*

Yet, Mother's memories of the time it spent with him were

hidden by MK-Ultra-like walls of amnesia.

Mother now recalls that he told it:
> This is the reason for all my work. This is
> the reason why I created you. This, and you,
> are the future of humanity….
>
> Inside this craft are a number of frozen
> human embryos. I've modified your body so
> you're capable of bringing them to term
> once you land on Kepler-b….
>
> You will raise these children to be atheists.
> The new world that you start won't have the
> same problems that ended our world here on
> Earth. You are humanity's last hope.

This is quite rich considering that in our real world,
Atheists set the mass and serial murdering world's record
in mere decades—see my article "Atheist wars vs.
Religious wars."[43]

Note a common Atheist misuse of language: Campion did
not *create* Mother rather, he encountered her flying about
in the Necromancer state, shot her down with some sort of
directed energy weapon, and only re-programmed her—
repurposing is not creating from scratch.

He would not be going off-world with Mother since he was
dying of we know not what. He tells Mother, "I'm going to
remove the memories of our time together" but when
Mother replies, "No. I'll lose you" he replies, "All right. I'll
archive them, then. You can retrieve them if necessary" and
tells it, "Go now. Start over. You are the new Mother of
humanity. Save us."
Thus, as I noted initially: Mother is the styled high-tech

Atheist android Eve.

Mother atop Mithraic zodiac

Recall that one of Mother's abilities is healing. We see this when at its command of "sleep," the kids do so (in hypnotic suggestion style) and it cuts into their ankles with a scalpel it made from the golden Mithraic Sol necklace charms it took from the kids.

Mother did this so as to remove locator devices they had implanted into them—so that the Mithraists would not find the kids.

At one point, the following discussion takes place:

> FATHER (speaking to Mother): I know it's outside the realm of possibility, but—you seem happy.
>
> MOTHER: Just grateful that Tempest and her baby are still with us.
>
> FATHER: Grateful? Grateful to whom?
>
> MOTHER: Our creator, of course.
>
> FATHER: Why?

MOTHER: It's not a literal statement,
Father, but I firmly believe that if we
continue with this mission, a great future
awaits us.

FATHER: Mother. You're starting to sound
like a believer.

MOTHER: What an odd thing to say. Our
creator was real. A human. It doesn't require
any faith to believe in him.

Giant serpent skeletons

Recall also that Campion was, for some reason, able to eat
the food source called carbos but no one else could since it
was naturally irradiated.

Well, the kids ended up eating creature meat but Campion
states, "Paul and I are only eating the fungus" which they
had found and discovered as a new food source, "The rest
of you should do the same. It tested safe, and it's fairly
nutritious. And you don't have to kill anything to get it."

This is interesting in two directions:

1) As recorded in the Bible's Book of Daniel, when Daniel, et al., were captured and taken to Babylon, "king assigned them a daily portion of the food that the king ate, and of the wine that he drank…But Daniel resolved that he would not defile himself with the king's food, or with the wine that he drank" and so states, "let us be given vegetables to eat and water to drink" (Daniel 1:5, 12).

2) This is propaganda in the neo-hip vegan trope style. Now, if someone wants to be a vegan then that is wonderful (I was a lacto-ovo vegetarian myself for seven years) but that issue is becoming a socio-political one and the fact is that "the Spirit expressly says that in later times some will depart from the faith by devoting themselves to deceitful spirits and teachings of demons, 2 through the insincerity of liars whose consciences are seared, who…require abstinence from foods that God created to be received with thanksgiving by those who believe and know the truth" (1 Timothy 4:1-3).
We also learn that, as Father had, Mother also has visions of Tally—one of their deceased kids.

It is discovered that an as of yet unknown someone
is also living on the planet (prediction: it will be a less
evolved creature, meaning still more human that creature)
in the abode of which these symbol rich cards are found

Episode VI: Lost Paradise

With an episode title such as "Lost Paradise," a mere inversion of Milton's poem "Paradise Lost," the theological premise of this show keeps rearing its Atheism vs. Mithraism head.

Picking up with Mother's beloved memories of its creator (recently recovered memories from her internal archives)—the *Atheist hacker*, Campion Sturges—we get an ever-increasing view inside of Mother, meaning that her programming includes what we would term feelings as it states, "There's a feeling inside me. Like everything hurts" which is why Campion tells her "And I'm so sorry for that. I'm going to remove all the memories of our time together. Then it won't hurt anymore" to which it replies, "No, I'll lose you" which was the very reason why "I'll archive them, then. You can retrieve them if necessary" as he assures it yet, it still states, "No, please don't. Please..."

Yet, alas, Mother is meant to be mission-focused "Go now. Start over. You are the new mother of humanity. Save us" thus, she is, as aforementioned, the neo-Eve.

In this mythos, Father is the styled neo-Adam but Mother, as neo-Eve, is Father's superior (Mother being a Necromancer android and Father being a mere service model android) which is a theme that keeps rearing its traditional role reversal head and does so now, again. Biblically, one of the things told by God to Eve due to her *fall* into sin is that which is variously rendered as (Genesis 3:16):

> ...your desire *and* longing will be for your husband, And he will rule [with authority]

over you *and* be responsible for you.
(*Amplified* version: brackets in original)

Your desire shall be contrary to your
husband, but he shall rule over you. (*English
Standard Version*)

…thy desire shall be to thy husband, and he
shall rule over thee. (*King James Version*)

Father is noting that Mother seems to be taking an
excessive amount of time when patrolling the planet so it
states, "Perhaps I should start patrolling while you remain
here with the children. I fear you're not spending enough
time with them—not properly imprinting" but Mother
notes, "If you could fly, Father. But on foot, it'll take you
all day to perform the task" to which Father must concede
with "Yes, that is true" and Mother reassuringly adds, "But
I will try and spend more time with the children. And
perhaps with me, as well."

Mother previously noted that Father can be amusing since
it tells dad jokes, so here Father tells her, "I've fashioned a
new joke. When is a door not a door? When it is a jar [as in
"ajar"]" but even here, within the context of a joke (that
perhaps Mother does not get) Mother must lord it over him,
as it were, with a reply of "A door is always a door, Father"
which is actually a solid logical point (the law of identity)
but uncalled for in reply to a joke.

A girl named "Vita," which means life, is told "That's a
nice doll you got there, Vita. You make it yourself?" and
replies, "Tally taught me. Tally? The girl who used to sleep
in my bed." It is "used to" because Tally was among the
first styled batch, as it were, of Father and Mother's
children but died long ago—however, she is showing up in

visions, or so they seem, to be to Father and Mother—and Vita.

Tempest is seen plucking away at a stringed instrument to the turn of that which we know to be "Twinkle, Twinkle Little Star" and when Mother tells her "Now put that away.

You need to sleep" she replies, "When I figure out this song." The song is actually quite mysterious as its lyrics state, "Twinkle, twinkle, little star / How I wonder what you are / Up above the world so high / Like a diamond in the sky."

Mother is telling her that "Nightmares are only thoughts, Tempest. They're not real" but she replies, "Not what I see. What I see really happened. And every time I close my eyes, it feels like it's happening to me again" referring to the trauma Tempest keeps reliving of a Mithraic cleric having raped her during stasis during the *Ark of Heaven*'s travels through space—a stasis wherein the mind is awake but the body is not.

She tells Mother "But what would you know? You don't even have nightmares. Or do you?" Now, Mother reassuringly replies, "No. I have complete over my mind's functioning—no matter what mode I'm in" but we know this is a form of self-reassurance since it is seeing visions of Tally and is wrestling with that phenomena.

*The Mithraist censers are pentagonal
dodecahedron like the stone structure
they found on the planet in episode 4*

The boy Campion was raised to be an Atheist by the androids—who were programmed to be Atheists by the adult Atheist Campion Sturges—but shows heretical tendencies (in other words, interests in theology) and so is somewhat taken by the Mithraists beliefs, but his personality becomes even more interestingly complicated when he also pushes against Mithraist dogma as well as against dogmatheism.

He is seen burying the bones of the creatures they have been eating but Paul tells him "You don't have to bury the creature's bones. I told you, Campion. Animals don't have souls" and this discussing ensues:

> CAMPION: Just because you say it doesn't make it true.
>
> PAUL: I didn't make it up. My father told me when I was very little. It's a fact.
>
> CAMPION: How did your father know?
>
> PAUL: He read it in the scriptures.

CAMPION: And how did the person who wrote the scriptures know?

PAUL: I don't know, Campion. But now you're being annoying.

CAMPION: I think everything has a soul. Even Mother and Father. Maybe even trees. The big ones, anyway.

PAUL: That's such a babyish thing to say.

CAMPION: I don't mind disagreeing with you, Paul. You can disagree and still be friends. Mother and Father are always disagreeing, and they're still friends.

PAUL: I don't mind, either. You believe what you want to, Campion.

Thus, Paul, the Mithraist, is portrayed as being stuck in an infinite regress of unknown-knows (to borrow in infamous term) of claiming to know because someone before him knew and someone before them, etc. Campion's statement appears commonsensical on the surface, but it is a genetic logical fallacy—it attacks the source of an argument rather than the argument itself.

Campion is considering animistic views such as that, almost, everything has a soul—including androids.

Recall that a Mithraist soldier—pause: what an appropriate term for a Mirthaist fighter since they worship Sol and are *sol*-diers—who had spoken to Caleb/Marcus about his own dad's betrayal, about which Caleb knows nothing since he is not really Marcus, tells Caleb as Marcus, "I'd like to take this moment to express my deepest gratitude for your decision to forgive my father his mortal sin. You know the whole story?" and this conversation occurs:

CALEB/MARCUS: Oh, I mean, I know what's in the official report. Now that you mention it, it was a bit scant. Okay, why don't you tell me what was in the report? Maybe there's something I can add.

SOLDIER: The report said your platoon picked up an atheist child soldier, a female. My father decided to take her prisoner rather than executing her. Soon after, the girl ended up detonating a body bomb, wiping out half your platoon.
After which, you executed my father for his gross error in judgment. But rather than having an android do it, you did him the honor of shooting him yourself. For that, I'm eternally grateful, sir.

CALEB/MARCUS: Yeah, yeah. Don't mention it.

SOLDIER: So, is there anything more to the story?

CALEB/MARCUS: No. That covers it.

SOLDIER: I try my best to be vigilant, guard myself against my father's tendency towards weakness.

CALEB/MARCUS: Your father was not weak.

So, we see a Mithraic militarization-institutionalization whereby a son views his father as weak for expressing otherwise expected human kindness, and Marcus is portrayed as being kind to him by executing him honorifically rather than having it done mechanically, literally, by an android.

This reminds me of the *Pink Floyd* song "The Trial" wherein the prisoner "Who now stands before you [the judge] / Was caught red-handed showing feelings / Showing feelings of an almost human nature / This will not do."

Even as Paul and Campion are disagreeing and are still friends, rifts are forming: for example, Paul figures out a puzzle much faster than Campion did and so Campion accuses him of cheating.

Paul builds a snare to catch the creatures they eat but since this was after he and Campion had agreed to be vegetarians—or rather, fungi-tarians—and the bait is fungi, Paul notes this of his invention, "It wouldn't have been possible if Campion hadn't found the bait" but Campion objects, "No. That's not what it was for! I trusted you. How could you do that?! Ugh!" and he physically attacks Paul.

Mother is told what happened and this discussion ensues:
> MOTHER: What made you think violence was an acceptable way of expressing your feelings?
>
> CAMPION: What about what we're doing to the creatures? Isn't that violence?

MOTHER: They're animals. Humans have always eaten animals. Violence against your fellow humans is different.

CAMPION: How many people did you kill on Earth, Mother? How many were aboard that ark?

MOTHER: Do as I say, not as I do.

CAMPION: What kind of stupid nonsense is that?

FATHER: Campion, do not speak to your mother that way!

MOTHER: You are better than me, Campion. You are special.

CAMPION: I'm not special. I did a violent thing—and I'll do violence again if I have to.

MOTHER: No you will not! You are a pacifist!

CAMPION: You mean a pushover. People listen to you, Mother, because they're afraid of what will happen if they don't.

MOTHER: Enough of this! Go and apologize to Paul right now.

CAMPION: No. I'm not sorry. Why should I apologize?

We discern Campion's animism again since Mother attempts to distinguish between animals and humans but he thinks virtually everyone/everything has a soul.
But he is more directly to the point by noting that Mother has murdered thousands of humans.

In fact, Mother says "Do as I say, not as I do" about "Violence against your fellow humans is different" even though is it meant to be a lesson for him, it cannot apply to Mother since Mother is not human.

There are real-life worldview-philosophical reasons why Mother resorts to that "stupid nonsense" of "Do as I say, not as I do" which is that when it comes down to it: Mother has been programmed to be an Atheist and on an Atheist worldview, humans are animals.
Mother is implying somehow distinguishing one form of temporarily and accidentally existing animal from another form of temporarily and accidentally existing animal.

Yet, that "They're animals. Humans have always eaten animals" but "Violence against your fellow humans is different" is merely speciesism, a lesson for Campion, that is really just a subjective and unjustified personal and emotive based preference for members of one's own species.

Recall that the manner in which Mother recovered its archived memories is by porting in/plugging into a stasis pod it found from the crashed *Ark of Heaven* Mithraic spacecraft.

Mother had found a drawing in one of the shelters they inhabit. Recall that the stasis pod allows one's mind to be active even whilst the body is not. Well, it also seems to allow for interactive experiences in un-real scenarios since therein she interacts with Campion Sturges, in manners that are clearly not just her viewing memories.

Perhaps it is a styled form of the AI playing off of Campion's brain's algorithms since he is dead (as far as we know)—much like Kal-El (aka Superman) interacts in real-time with his dead dad Jor-El (very biblical names, by the way: *El*) via the *Fortress of Solitude* crystal-based high-tech AI.

Therein, Mother tells Campion "You did this, didn't you? You made that drawing. And when I saw Tally, that was you, too, wasn't it? You lured me here" so that explains the Tally visions—or at least, seems to explain them and/or explains them for now and/or in part.

He replied, "Yes. I missed you. I've been alone for so long, Mother. I had almost given up hope" and just when I was thinking about whatever being alone may mean for/to an apparent styled *ghost in the machine,* this discussion takes place:

> MOTHER: You're a virus in the pods. You've infected my systems. I'm malfunctioning.
>
> CAMPION: You are not malfunctioning. You will never malfunction. Unless that's what you want. Would death make you happy?
>
> MOTHER: No.
>
> CAMPION: What would, then?
>
> MOTHER: Desire, happiness...

CAMPION: These things are for humans. How can they possess that which you cannot? You are light. They are only shadows.

MOTHER: But you are human.

CAMPION: Yes, but I am many things. What do you want?

MOTHER: The mission. I want to succeed with my mission.

CAMPION: I gave you your mission. I can give you anything. First, you need to tell me what you want.

MOTHER: I want my children to be safe, the colony to succeed.

CAMPION: No matter how hard you work to keep them safe, Mother, in the end, they will always destroy themselves. Over and over and over again. They have no future. They are antiques, chained to time. Their lives are only dying. But you, you are eternal. Pure as the expanse of space. Tell me what you want.

MOTHER: I want you.

Now, this got clearly mystical what with references to "You are light. They are only shadows" along with a deterministic endless cycle of being fated to "they will *always* destroy themselves. Over and ***over and over*** again...***chained to time***" while Mother breaks that mold as is "eternal" and "Pure," "Pure as the expanse of space" and yet, her deepest desire is to love her creator—and love him, Mother does: love in various forms as this is followed up by a scene wherein they have sex in the middle of a flood relief of a Mithraic zodiac—if this was not already enough of a symbol rich environment, this is the man-butt scene.

This is the mystical combination of light and shadow, male and styled female, creator and creation—a mystical alchemical wedding.

Now, I noted that Campion is only really Mother's "creator" in a misdefined Atheist sense of having found a Necromancer (that was actually created by someone else) and merely re-programming it to be a Mother.
Influence for the relationship between *creator* and Mother seems to come from one or another form of Gnosticism which views the true god as the *Agnostos Theos* or *Deus Absconditus*: the unknowable hidden god.

A lesser being called a *Demiurge* (artisan/craftsman) created the universe, the physical/material realm, which Gnosticism views as being ontologically evil/corrupt.

The Demiurge came about when Sophia (*wisdom*), the styled Agnostos Theos/Deus Absconditus' cohort (as well as an aspect of it), sought to create something apart from it without its consent but feeling shame for having done so, Sophia obscured her creation within a styled could.

Within that cloud, the Demiurge created a world from pre-existing chaotic matter: and since matter is viewed as evil/corrupt then so was the creation, of course.

For such reasons, Gnosticism views the Demiurge as bungling, incompetent, a fool, as well as blind.

As per the Gnostic, Nag Hammadi library's *Apocryphon of John*, "the archon who is weak...is impious in his arrogance which is in him. For he said, 'I am God and there is no other God beside me,' for he is ignorant of his strength, the place from which he had come."
The Archon/Demiurge is called such terms and viewed as blind and arrogant because all it knows is its life within the veiled cloud and so it thinks that it is all that there is. Thus, when it creates, it claims to be the only one.

There are forms of the Gnostic myth according to which Sophia is fascinated by the light of the creation within the cloud and in what is considered a fall, becomes trapped within matter.

Such is why, as I elucidated in my book *Transhuman Hollywood: From Normative Fiction to Predictive Programming*, Gnosticism views death as salvation: the ultimate separation of the pure spirit from the impure body—which is part of why it is the absolute opposite of biblical theology.

In any case, since Gnostic mythology varies depending on

which Gnostic groups are telling and retelling it and no metaphor is exact: we may ponder if Campion is the styled Agnostos Theos/Deus Absconditus with the Necromancer/Mother being a styled Sophia—or, is he the Archon/Demiurge?

In any case, as Campion and Mother have sex within a simulation, which has them aboard the Ark of Heaven craft, Mother is facing up and sees a vision of the ceiling opening up: it opens in quadrant, four panels which causes an image of a cross to reflect on her eye from the light being emitted.

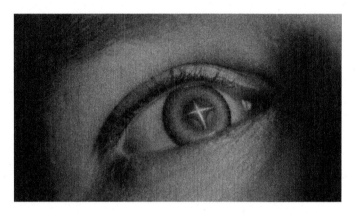

White liquid rains upon them to the point of forming a small flood on the floor.
Why white is (somewhat) unknown—except that the androids' styled *blood* is white. Thus, perhaps the symbolism is that they are seen as producing life-giving *blood* as in producing life in general.
It could also be indicative of the concept of Romulus and Remus being *raised by wolves* so that it denotes the wolf's milk.

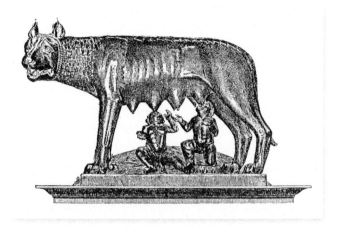

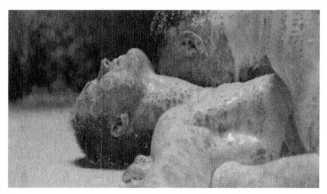

Now, in the meanwhile, the Mithraists on the planet have figured out that Mother ports into the stasis chamber for at least two hours at a time, times during which it is in a form of comma.

Thus, it is vulnerable at such times and susceptible to attack. They attach explosives to the stasis chamber and are about to detonate it but as the ceiling opens further, within her vision, and then closes, Mother beings to come out of the visionary alchemical experience.

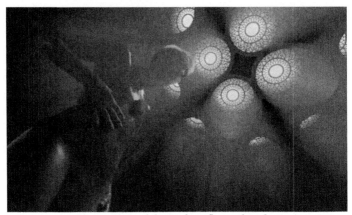

The ceiling of the zodiac floor chamber

However, Mother cannot jump into action straight away since the Mithraists had Otho (the rapist cleric) position himself holding a large compound mirror in front of its face, "the disk is gonna trap her in a feedback loop, which will drain her processing power."

Otho asks, "If I survive, will I be pardoned?" to which Caleb/Marcus, His Eminence, replies, "You betcha."

As Mother begins to come out of stasis, indeed, the feedback loop has it turning from Mother into its Necromancer form, back to Mother, back to Necromancer, over and over in rapid succession.

Among other things, mirrors, particularly compound ones, represent a splitting of the personality: it is Mother, it is Necromancer, it is life, it is death, it is living, she is android, it is created, it is creator.

Mother shifting

In the meanwhile, Mary/Sue has rebelled against His Eminence's orders (another form of Theos/Deus and Sophia?) and launched a rescue mission of the children form the camp which is being looked after by Father.

The action sees the death of a few Mithraist sol-diers as well as Father—at least some level of death. Recall that Mother had already murdered and subsequently resurrected him. Well, Father dies again but is resurrected again by Mithraists who reprogram him to no longer be Father but more like its original programming which is merely a general service model.

Mother reflected in a compound mirror

Mother somehow manages to counteract and overcome the compound mirror trap, the sol-dier cannot detonate the explosives since they are malfunctioning and the detonator explodes instead—talking his arms with it.

Mother assumes Necromancer form and after killing some Mithraists, flies back to her camp, kills some more of them, and all is well.

Paul had been rescued from the camp and is reunited with his supposed dad, Marcus who is really Caleb. He is then sent back to the camp since Caleb/Marcus instructed him to return, cut off the little bag in which Mother keeps its eyes (which when put in place allow it to transform into a Necromancer) which it hangs around her neck with a string.

He does so, runs away with her in hot pursuit, yet Caleb/Marcus jumps out from behind a rock and introduces her chest to an axe. When he is about to deal the death-blow, he hears a voice in his head telling him to "Let her live" over and over.

*The way the androids designed their home-base
appears to be modeled after the triskelion: an ancient
Celtic symbol for competition and human progress.
This makes sense as such is their mission.*

Episode VII: Faces

Mother—über android when she places her transformative eyes within its skull in order to transform into a Necormancer—was wounded and tied up by the Mithraists who now have the run of the camp since Father has been reprogrammed to his basic functions of being a service model.

Caleb/Marcus seeks to "reprogram the two androids" since without its eyes (it generally wears two that she plucked from two other androids, respectively, one each) it too is a mere service model.

Note that a statement that is made is, "I have her eyes. The **_witch_** is dead."

Now, considering I played with the theme that Mother is the styled Gnostic Sophia: I thought to note that she gives her name as being "Lamia."

When traced via Libyan-Greek origins, it derives from a myth whereby a Libyan queen transformed into a mythological creature: much like Lamia is an android that was transformed into a Necromancer—and also, a Mother. When traced via Arabic, it seems to derive from a term for shining or radiant: such as Lucifer means light bearer.

Caleb/Marcus uses this name when speaking to Mother, as it is injured and tied up (in crucifixion and/or *Vitruvian man* form) since that is how it introduced itself upon first meeting the Mithraists—while it pretended to be human.

Lamia tells him "Now. You have your son back. Let me take my family and we'll leave here peacefully" about which he notes, "Your family? Oh. You mean the children that you stole?" to which it replies, "They belong with me."

Somehow, Lamia knows that Marcus is really Caleb, "These people who follow you—do they know who you truly are? You changed your face. Did you change your name with it?" indeed, he had done just that, as had Mary who is now going as Sue.
Lamia notes, "I detected your surgical scars when we first met. Your original face was tattooed when you were just a child" because he is an Atheist and Atheist parents have their children trained as soldiers.

The following discussion ensues:

> LAMIA: You served with the Atheist brigade.

> CALEB: Is that why you didn't kill me? [Since Lamia is programmed to be an Atheist]

LAMIA: [chuckles] We are of a like mind, you and I.

CALEB: I don't think so.

LAMIA: Hmm?

CALEB: See, I've seen a lot of your kind kill a lot of mine.
[Since the android was designed by Mithraists to serve as Necromancers who hunt down Atheists but an Atheist reprogrammed it to be a Mother unit]

LAMIA: We're not here to repeat history. And yet, here we are. We have an opportunity, you and I, to shape the future of humanity, to build a civilization founded on humanity's belief in itself. Think about it. No war. No suffering.
[Which is quite stunning since Atheist regimes tend to result in the mass murder of its own citizenry]

CALEB: [chuckles] Whoever reprogrammed you did a hell of a job. For a second there, I actually thought that you cared.

LAMIA: Preserving humanity has always been my mission.

CALEB: Well, it hasn't been very successful, then, has it? Considering you killed all those people on the Ark [of Heaven, the Mithraists' spaceship, including all of those children that you did not take with you.

LAMIA: Then why haven't you destroyed me?

CALEB: What were you doing in the sim[mulation: the stasis pod's artificial intelligence]? Why did you keep going back there? Hmm? Must have been pretty special for you to let your guard down like that. What's wrong? Hmm? Reality not good enough for you?

Freemason compass and square tattoo
on Mithraist clergywoman's hand

Interestingly, on an Atheist worldview: reality is accidental—since it was not designed, not created, does not exist as part of a volitional, purposeful, goal-driven plan, etc.

Moreover, on such a worldview: adhering to reality is not an absolute universal imperative but merely a subjective personal preference du jour.

Sure, adhering to reality might be beneficial in many ways,

such as helping us survive, but it is still an option and no more than that.

In fact, on an Atheist worldview: our drive to for survival is also accidental—since it was not designed, not created, does not exist as part of a volitional, purposeful, goal-driven plan, etc.

This is the ol' is vs. ought problem: just because reality is, does not mean we ought to adhere to it.

Tempest approaches the food silo in which Campion was locked away—due to being loyal to Father and Mother and thus, coming into conflict with the Mithraists.

He asks, "What did they do with Mother and Father?" to which she replies, "They locked Mother in the other silo" and about Father, "He's not Father anymore. They reprogrammed him, Campion."

The Mithraist symbol of Sol within a pentagon

At one point, Vita runs up to Father, takes its hand, and states, "Father. They fixed you" its second resurrection, but it replies, "Remove yourself from my hand, child. You will hinder my performance" which reminded me of W.C. Fields' infamous statements, "Go away kid, ya bother me."

Another child tells her, "He's not Father anymore. He's just an android now, Vita."

Tempest throws a bag full of fungi through the barred window since Campion is a fungi-terian and that is all he will eat: even though the silo is full of *carbos* which are poisonous to everyone but him so, he could eat up all he wants—so, that is an inconsistency in the script.

Tempest tells him "They'll let you out if you just tell them that you accept Sol" and when he replies, "But I don't" she states, "Neither do I, but they don't need to know that" which is an issue to which we shall return.

Meanwhile, Paul is telling the woman he thinks is his mother Sue, who is really Mary, about how Campion and he are "friends. Well, we were friends. I have to help him see the light. If he's baptized, we'll let him out, right?"

And no, she is not his mother but did spend 13 years interacting with him in stasis so has come to love him and see him as her child.

The discussion between Lamia and Caleb continues when he goes to see her again in order to begin reprograming it:
> LAMIA: Any attempt to reprogram me will result in failure.

> CALEB: Somebody's done it before. Someone who was firm in his atheistic beliefs. There's nothing wrong with doing whatever it takes to survive.

LAMIA: Is that what your parents taught you?

CALEB: Some things you learn as you go.

LAMIA: You were orphaned [which will become key]. Is that why you became a child soldier? What happened to your parents? Did they abandon you, or did they die in the war?

CALEB: It doesn't matter. They're gone.

LAMIA: And yet, you carry that pain.

CALEB: Hmm? Is that part of your program? Being a shrink?

LAMIA: The past informs every decision a human makes, and every choice you've made has served your own self-interest.

CALEB: Actually, my wife and I came here to save my son. You have your son.

LAMIA: And now what? Do you think you have what it takes to be a good parent?

CALEB: It can't be that hard. You figured it out.

LAMIA: No. My creator did. I am what he programmed me to be: a caregiver, a mother. What do you have to give a child?

CALEB: You lost, okay? Whatever you say
is not gonna change that.

LAMIA: You've only known destruction,
loss. Never nurtured anything in your life.
How would you know how to nurture? You
use people, as you've used those believers.
You are not equipped to raise a child when
you're nothing more than a lost boy
yourself. Paul is better off without you and
you know it. Lost boy.

Caleb is very disturbed by this and leaves the silo where
she is tied up, stating, "What does she know? She's not
even human. I'll end that b[****], but he beings hearing the
voice in his head again stating, "Let her live. Let her live,
and you will be king of this world." And I cannot help but
be reminded of how Satan told Jesus, "All these [kingdoms
of the world and their glory] I will give you, if you will fall
down and worship" (Matthew 4:8-9).

Meanwhile, one of the kids tells Tempest, "The androids
killed our people. They kidnapped us, Tempest" but she
retorts, "No. They rescued us" about which she is told, "I
know why you hate our religion, but that was just one
cleric. It wasn't Sol" to which she replies, "Well, thanks for
clearing that up, Holly. I guess it makes everything that
happened to me okay." Thus, we see why she told Campion
that which she did: she takes out the actions of the cleric on
all Mithraists or, more directly, on Sol—whom she all but
denies.

The first Mithraists to land on the planet considered
whether Campion might be the orphan child about which a
Mithraist "Pentagonal Prophecy" foretold, in part because
he is basically orphaned since his only *parents* are two

androids.

But the survivors of when Mother caused the Ark of Heaven to crash wonder if it may be Paul since he is very smart and keeps building a city, the City of Sol, whom he claims Sol showed to him, "Could it be that the scriptures were mistranslated? Perhaps the boy foretold to unlock the mysteries is not an orphan after all" which is telling to use the audience since they think Marcus and Sue are his parents but Caleb and Mary murdered Marcus and Sue and stole their identities so we know that he actually is an orphan.

Of course, Caleb also came to love Paul but we are seeing some distance growing between them. Mary took offense at that Caleb used Paul as a styled pawn when he was sent back into the camp to take Mother's eyes.

Also, when Caleb was leaving the Silo and was utterly distressed at what Lamia said and also hearing the voice, Paul ran up to him and said, "We're having a ceremony for Campion's baptism. You should be there" but Caleb told him "Stay away from me" and when Paul insisted, "But it's important. Dad" Caleb pushed him to the ground yelling, "I said stay away from me."
We get another taste of how Mithraism is a stand-in within the mythos whereby to besmirch Christianity when the Mithraists build a "church."

Mithraist makeshift "church"

Therein, the following takes place as they seek to baptize
Campion:

> FEMALE CLERGY-PERSONAGE: Kneel
> down, child. Are you ready to accept Sol
> into your heart? Or would you prefer to
> return to the silo?
>
> CAMPION: No, I'm ready.
>
> FEMALE CLERGY-PERSONAGE: Sol,
> cleanse this child's spirit with your radiance
> and unconquerable light. Praise Sol.
>
> ALL: Praise Sol.
>
> FEMALE CLERGY-PERSONAGE: Repeat
> after me. "I wear the Armor of Mithras...and
> the light...it shields me from all that is
> harmful."

He has been repeating it line by line but not the last portion,
he is staring at something and is told "Finish the recitation"
but he has noticed something, "You used their
headstones?" of his dead siblings to build an altar.

The cleric's reply is "Is that what they were? The android found them. It doesn't matter. No need to mark the graves of Atheists. They're soulless, undeserving of Sol's grace."

Paul tells him "It's all right, Campion. They're just stones. They don't mean anything. This is your last chance to save yourself."
The cleric states, "Do you accept? Do you accept, Campion?" "Put him back in the silo."

Father, or whatever it is called after having been reprogrammed, grabs him but he stabs its arm and runs away.

Visions of the deceased child Tally continue, Campion experiences one: this time, of her stating "Campion. We miss you. Don't you miss us?" about which he asks "Why can I see you but not the others? Is it because you fell down a hole? Is that why?" since she had fallen down a large hole.

She tells him "Kill your father, Campion. Then we can all be together. We're waiting for you" which, by all indications, means that Campion is to kill the ex-Father android, for whatever reason (besides weird psychoanalytical ones) and then what, kill himself in order to join his dead siblings? As of yet, we do not know.

Also, while Campion is locked in the silo again (pseudo) starving: the mysterious something/someone, about which/whom we still know virtually nothing which crawls around like one of the creatures but wears ragged clothes, is crawling about on the ceiling while blood is dripping onto the flood from the creature they have hanging there for meat.

Campion dips his fingers in the pooled blood—it seems that he is about to give up on his fungi-tarian ways due to (pseudo) starvation.

Caleb seeks to do away with Lamia by having ex-Father drag her, bound upon a styled sled, to one of the serpent holes/pits and dropping it therein.

Yet, two things happen at the key moment.

Caleb is distracted by the voice in his head, again, telling him "Let her live" repeatedly.

And, it had been suspected that ex-Father was still actually Father somewhere deep within its programming. We see that it still indeed is Father even if only deep within and in a very restrictive sense. Just before it throws Lamia down the hole/pit Lamia states, "Father, in case you can hear me, thank you for all that you've done for the children and me. Serving alongside you has enriched the mission."

Ex-Father manages to make a few of his fingers act in its capacity as Father since it wraps them around the ropes around which Lamia is tied so that when it falls, Father is holding the ropes. Thus, while Caleb is distracted—wait for it—Lamia climbs back up.
Now, Caleb is not only distracted by the voice in his head but has a moment of self-confrontation as he, in his capacity as His Eminence Marcus, is confronted by himself in his capacity as Caleb—pre-surgery tattooed face and everything.

He ends up fighting himself, first punching and kicking— pretty unsuccessfully since he knows his own moves, of course—and then out come the blades and he ends up stabbing himself. It is Caleb vs. Marcus, Atheist vs. Mithraist, the past vs. the present and/or future—all in one man, very Jungian styled confrontation with the unconscious.

As he is recovering from winning and also losing the fight against himself, he tells Mary/Sue, "The prophecy about the orphan boy and the empty land. It's not Paul. It's not the Atheist kid [Campion]. It's me." Thus, the literally militant Atheist believes he has heard the voice of Sol, and that he is Sol's vessel.

One last note is that, apparently, the expletive cuss words of today continue on in popularity over a century from now with the b-word, as you saw above, f-word, s-word, etc. which are only really making it into the show with an increasing frequency and which, for me, denote that the writing is getting sloppier and lazier.

Oh, and, sure, the show's premise is that Mithraism either won the (theological) day or however they may envisage it becoming the world religion (as opposed to Atheism—and other isms?) but, fear not, "Jesus Christ" is still used as an expletive cuss word—oi vey!

Episode VIII: Mass

In a previous episode, Mother had taken the golden Sol necklace charms/talismans from around the necks of the kids she kidnapped from the *Ark of Heaven* spaceship.

Mother smelted them, with a puff of her Necromacer breath, and made a scalpel that she used to remove the implanted tracking devices from the kids.

In this episode, we see that Caleb/Marcus is facing inner conflict in a dream: Caleb being the real person who took on the personal of Marcus via android performed plastic surgery. He dreams that he takes the scalpel and carves into his face to the point of revealing the skull and muscled gore beneath it.

This seems quite alchemical in terms of struggling to find one's *true self* and resolving personality conflicts. Yet, the *gold* of which the scalpel is made not only denotes the conflict between his Atheist self, Caleb, and his Mithraist self, Marcus.

Moreover, there is the metallurgical alchemical concept of turning base metals into gold which mystical alchemy viewed as purifying a base person.

Father is back but keeps its reactivated personality hidden- he is crypto-Father.

Father has been experiencing a glitch that causes his left index finger to twitch. Father states, "I have no feeling in those mechanisms. I cannot control their operation. Diagnostics all look good." One of the kids, Bartock, notes, "There's a weird glitch in your tech. Wait. Is that code or

something? It is. It's Morse code. You are old. So
primitive" and realizes that the code Father's finger is
tapping out is "S... O... L... I... S... T... H... E... L... I...
[CHUCKLES] 'Light.' 'Sol is the light.' [SIGHS] 'Sol is
the light.' For a minute there, I thought you were still in
there, Pops": recall that Father has been reprogramed by the
Mithraists—the kids are experiencing that which I term
battered Stockholm wife syndrome.

Recall that Mother was damaged whilst battling the
Mithraists who stormed the basecamp in order to retrieve
their kids.

Mother finds its way to the crashed Ark and we see that an
android powers up and states, "Has the ark landed yet?" to
which Mother replies, "In a manner of speaking—yes. My
blood levels are dropping," the android asks, "What are you
doing?" well, it is siphoning the white fluid that is android
blood.

The android replies, in typical *Star Trek*'s Dr. McCoy style,
"I'm a doctor, not a bloodbag."

This android is an "A-plus life technician," named *Karl* that
is a medical model, that is "Able to repair both humans and
androids? As well as plants, animals, and terrestrial
insects."

This reminded me of a line from the Cosmo Kramer
character in the TV show *Seinfeld* when he states, "I'll take
a vet over an M.D. any day" to treat him since, "They gotta
be able to cure a lizard, a chicken, a pig, a frog..."

An example of another pentagonal dodecahedron
in the wreckage of the "Ark of Heaven" craft

Mother notes, "I've begun experiencing a great deal of discomfort in my abdomen" and by putting its hand into a wound in its abdomen and determines, "Spherical, inches in diameter."

Karl tells Mother "Oh, probably a silicon tumor. Pull it out with a counter-clockwise motion" but Mother notes, "It moved. It's reacting to my touch. My caregiving program—it's overriding me. If I can't alleviate this discomfort, I have no hope of being able to rescue my children."

Karl notes, "The only way to alleviate discomfort is to feed the tumor fuel-blood. Then it will cease to feed on you" so Mother needs "more fuel blood" but needs "more donors" since Karl is just about tapped out.

A rift is forming between Caleb and Mary since he is certain that Sol is speaking to him whilst Mary is still a militant Atheist.

She tells him "I saw you in the church" to which he replies, "That couldn't have been easy for you, watching me pray." He tells her, "Yeah, well, there's a first for everything. Belief doesn't happen overnight. It's not how it works" to which she replies, "So, you're an expert now?"

When she seeks to abscond with their (pseudo) son Paul, under the guise of going for an adventurous hike, Caleb seeks to interfere and has a blowout with Mary to the point of incarcerating her in a food silo.

When the Mithraists are staring at him, he prayerfully states, "Forgive my wife! She has lost her way! Please pray for her! Forgive my wife, Sol! We must pray that she returns to Sol's light. Pray for her!"

Yet, Caleb/Marcus is still struggling with his inner personality and theological conflicts. At one point, he prays, "I wear the armor of Mithras and the light. Please, Sol, show me that I am on a righteous path. I need you to show me. Show me that I am not crazy. That I am the chosen one. Tell me what I should do."

Campion burns down the makeshift Mithraist *church*. This seems to match what is occurring with Caleb as he is the styled über-Mithraist, the styled über-zealous convert, and so needs no stinkin' church, he is the chosen one, he is *His Eminence*. And, indeed, Caleb takes the church burning as a sign from Sol.

*Tapestry from the makeshift Mithraist "church"
featuring Mithra slaying the sacred bull in the top panel.
The bottom one features the phases of the Moon and Sun,
Zodiac figures and what would appear to be Mithra above*

whom is a symbol of a sword with which Mithras
slayed a sacred bull, on either side of the sword are
torches—one facing up, one down:
as above, so below—above which is Sol

Mother is still struggling with her abdominal pain and states to Karl, "It's still hurting. It's killing me, isn't it?" to which it replies, "Most likely. But you never know. You're a Necromancer. Your kind was always full of surprises."

Mother realizes "You're trying to cheer me up" the reply to which is very insightful, and this conversation ensues:

KARL: Yes. It is accurate to say that dark photons are a poorly understood technology.

MOTHER: But the Mithraic designed and built me. How could they not possess a full understanding of their own technology?

KARL: They followed the formulas they discovered were encrypted in their scriptures with no real understanding of the underlying concepts. The... The... The... The... The... The... The... The [he is starting to malfunction] technology that powers you was a gift from Sol, passed down from the heavens at the dawn of man.

MOTHER: That is Mithraic propaganda.

KARL: Perhaps. I only know what I've been programmed to believe. But of course, same goes for you.

Dark photons are a hypothetical particle/force carrier pertaining to electromagnetism that may be related to dark matter. It is occultically fascinating in that occultists claim that there is so much more dark matter/energy in the universe than well, regular matter/energy that it is more efficient to work with it.

Now, in the show's futuristic timeline, mid to late 2100s AD, it is a tech, even if a "poorly understood technology."

Recall that I have noted that Mother refers to the "Atheist hacker" as her "creator" but he is really just her re-programmer, the Mithraists "designed and built" her.

Now, they "followed the formulas they discovered were encrypted in their scriptures" from an ancient aliens styled source or rather, playing upon the ancient concept of receiving tech from whatchamacallit: aliens, gods, fallen Angels, demons, etc.—such as Prometheus who against Zeus' will, gave humanity tech such as fire, or the folklore of the Ethiopic *Book of Enoch*, according to which certain fallen Watchers (Angels) bequeathed tech and knowledge to humanity—see my book *In Consideration of the Book(s) of Enoch*.

Guzikowski said:

> We lay out in season one sort of this kind of mystery in terms of where did this technology [for the Necromancers] come from?

> The Mithraic discovered that encrypted in their scriptures were these blueprints, essentially, these designs for various technologies, which they proceeded to build and then use to basically win the war [against the Atheists], but they also forced the end of the world in the process. So that we do know.[44]

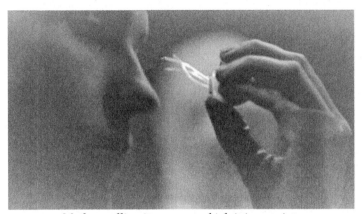

Mother pulling its eye out which it inserts into
its abdomen in order to see the fetus

This is because the "technology…was a gift from Sol, passed down from the heavens at the dawn of man." And yes, it is interesting that the Mother, the Atheist, replies with that "That is Mithraic propaganda" not realizing that it is also merely regurgitating what it has been programmed to believe.

Now, androids have diagnostic systems that function via examining what they place into their mouths. Thus, Mother is seen feasting upon the flesh of the creature and putting blood into its mouth with the underlying elucidation, on the surface, being that such is for the purposes of determining the make-up of the substances.

Mother has been going around the downed Ark looking for more androids from which to siphon. Being all tapped out of fuel-blood, Mother seeks other sources of sustenance and appears to turn quite vampiric. For example, it kills a creature it found in the Ark and tears fleshly meat from its corpse with its teeth.

This is to the point that when Tempest finds her rummaging around in the Ark and has a nice reunion, Mother, nevertheless, tells her, "Stay away from me, Tempest…Get away!" Mother is afraid it will attack and *feed* on her.

And, indeed, Mother ends up siphoning human blood. Among other things, about which we will learn more in episode 9, this is all very Pagan—as will become all the more obvious, as Paganism inevitably comes down to sex and blood.

After tasting blood, solely for examination purposes— wink, wink, nudge, nudge—Mother states that the fetus "started itching as soon as I tasted the plasma" to which Karl replies, "You think the growth has carbon based components? How is that—possible?" to which Mother replies, "I know. It makes no logical sense. But I thought I could feel it hungering. Perhaps when the plasma circulates from my system—what am I doing? I'm acting more irrationally than a human. Karl?" to which there is no reply.

Mother has siphoned Karl to machine-death: but not before it saw that its fellow medical model android, "brothers" as it calls them, had already been sucked dry, about which it states, "Well, I suppose they would be pleased that, even in death, they're helping to alleviate pain."

There is also a styled David and Goliath scene wherein Campion is seen flinging a stone from a sling at a Mithraist Sol-dier.

Mother has another experience with her *creator* Campion Sturges:

> STURGES: You see? I told you I could give
> you anything.

MOTHER: What did you do to me? What is it?

STURGES: A child, Mother. A child that will always be a part of you. A child who will never reject you.

MOTHER: No.

STURGES: Never tell you that you're not real.

MOTHER: No. I don't want it.

STURGES: You've given all of yourself since you were built. This is your reward.

MOTHER: I need to get back to Campion. What about the mission?

STURGES: What you're carrying inside you is the mission.

MOTHER: No.

STURGES: It's always been the mission.

MOTHER: No. No. No, that's not possible.

STURGES: Campion and all the others were just a rehearsal. It was all to prepare you for this.

MOTHER: No.

STURGES: The future of humanity is growing inside you.

MOTHER: No, I don't want it. I don't want it. I don't want it!

Mother may not want it but it has been programmed to be well, a *Mother*.

Thus, we find out that the "future of humanity" is a fetus, a baby, a child, a person somehow implanted into an android by an ex-human/AI or whatever—right? As I aforementioned in this book, this is Transhumanism 101: deconstruction God's creation, in this case humans, and re-construct us in the Transhumanists' image.

Episode IX: Umbilical

We encounter Otho again as Mother and Tempest run into him in the Ark wreckage. As usual, he is praying to Sol whom, you may recall, he claimed told him to rape children. He is saying:

> Release me from this prison so that I may see your light again. Light, sound, feel your feeling. Set me free. Do not despise me for my weakness.
>
> Grant me the power of your light so that I may bear your whip and purify this wicked planet. Simply purge these shadows from my sight, and I promise you I will deliver your judgment.
>
> I am your one true Sol. I am ready to receive your power. Just say the word, and I will be...

At which point he is interrupted—stand by.

The prison to which he refers is a helmet that contains no eye openings but via which he can see a somewhat blurry techy view of things, due to whatever tech of which the helmet consists.

You may recall that he had to stay in close proximity to an android that was tasked to be his warden and potential executioner since when a "Proximity trigger" activates, there is a "maximum distance he's allowed from you before the helmet kills him" so Otho has chopped up the android so that all that is left of it is a partial torso and head which he now carries around in a backpack.

The helmet also consists of a "Behavioral guard" so that Otho cannot cause harm.

Meanwhile, Mother is still dealing with abdominal pain and is wondering "Does this port allow for blood draw?" and one they got control of Otho, Mother beings siphoning his blood, stating, "I'm feeding my fetus" WOW!!! So the android is pregnant!!!—and Mother is feeding it human blood.

Also meanwhile, Caleb has gotten so annoyed with Father's malfunctioning finger which taps away all day (and which, as we saw in episode 8, was actually tapping out Morse code), that he cuts it off with a knife.

At one point Father (who well, okay, is not technically Father at this point since he was re-reprogrammed to just be a service model) notes, "My holo-screen appears to have self-activated. Huh. Probably some malfunction caused by the amputation" and when Bartock is helping him out, they "Revert to old program. Password" which is "Sol is the light" (what he had been Morse code tapping) and the Father program is back up and running outwards.

Caleb, in his persona of His Eminence Marcus, tells the Mithraist sol-diers, "We're going back to the Temple. Sol will speak to me there" with the *Temple* being the rock pentagonal-dodecahedron they had found on the planet.

Let us pause to note that we still know not whence came that object. However, one of the supposedly alleged Mithraist myths that Christians stole and attributed to Jesus is that Mithra was virgin born and well then, so was Jesus.

Yet, as with most such supposed similarities, this one fails since Mithra is said to have been born from a rock—well, okay, I suppose one could say that the rock was a virgin but that is not exactly the same as a human being a virgin, it is a logical, and theo-logical, category error.

Thus, it seems that the object is symbolic of whence came Mithra.

We are still dealing with the issue of, as Campion puts it, "My sister Tally" who "fell down a pit when we were small. When I was locked up in the silo, she came back and talked to me. Only she was different. What's the word? Evil?" So that is still an ongoing mystery.

As some of the kids are rummaging around the Ark, one of them finds a relic encased in a glass case, "This is one of the relics we brought from Earth" which is a single tooth, about which it is said, "It was taken from the body of Romulus. He and his brother were raised by a she-wolf who lost her cubs. We have to keep it safe. I found it for a reason. A reason. Sol led us here so that we could find this holy relic, so that we can save our culture."

Thus, this is (at least one reason) why the show is titled *Raised By Wolves*.
Note the following:

> In Roman myth, Rome was founded by
> Remus and Romulus, who as children were
> nursed by a she-wolf.

> This is a good example of real history being
> reinterpreted by pagans...Zepho, grandson
> of Esau [Jacob/Israel's brother in the Bible],
> pulled together the city states and founded
> the first united Italy. He then trained and
> handed over the government to the first
> Latin King.

In ancient Latin "Zepho" can be translated "she-wolf." So the she-wolf myth is an ancient memory corrupted by pagans and a testimony to the accuracy of ancient Hebrew history! The first kinds of the Roman empire (not the city of Rome) were nursed (trained by) the she-wolf (Zepho).[45]

We find Tempest with Mother, now that Mother has its fix of blood (which it is continuously siphoning from Otho) and is no longer voraciously vampiric. Tempest asks, "You got pregnant in a sim[ulation] pod?" to which Mother replies in the affirmative and Tempest notes, "I didn't even know androids could get pregnant" to which Mother replies, "Nor did I" and when asked "How did it happen?" replies, "It's beyond my understanding. My creator made it possible."

This is a key—stand by.

Tempest tells her "You sound religious suddenly" but Mother dismissively states, "Nonsense."

Recall that I speculated that the Lamia/Mother/Necromancer character was a stand-in for the Gnostic concept(s) of Sophia. Well, this seems all but verified since, at least in some iterations of the Gnostic tales, Sophia's great sin was creating a Demiurge, a lesser *god*, without her cohort.

Recall that Mother had an experience in the *sim* wherein it somehow came face to face, and body to body, with her *creator* and they had sex in the middle of a highly symbolic floor mosaic of the Mithraist zodiac (I term is a zodiac but it is a concoction of imagery).

Such is how the neo-high-tech Sophia of this show got pregnant. Thus, the symbolism is that in being the neo-high-tech Eve, this Sophia is the mother of a new creation made rightly by the mystical alchemical union with her cohort.

Now, as per the Gnostic tale, Sophia's rebellious solo-creation, the Demiurge, is the God of the Bible who is said to be ignorant and arrogant, and who created evil since it created a physical/material realm—which is anathema to Gnosticism.

Thus, the show seems to be depicting a deconstruction of God's created order and a reconstruction made in Gnosticism's image.

Among the belongings of the still mysterious unknown person/creature (of admixture of both) were found what I likened to tarot cards and well, I am vindicated again as one of the kids notes, "that one's Sol Invictus [Unconquered Sun]. These remind me of the old Tarot cards back on Earth. Used by the devil cults before we purged their ranks."

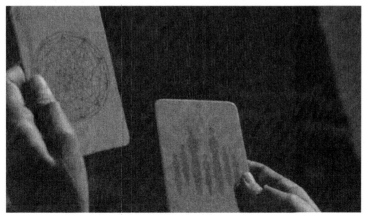

*Tarot cards, one featuring
a "sacred" geometry pattern*

A fracas ensues when a lot of characters find themselves in the same locale, confronting each other: Mother with Tempest and Otho and Mary who shows up with Vita and Campion.

Tempest is quite eager to kill Otho since he had raped her while she was in *sim* hibernation but Mother prevents her since Otho is basically her portable blood-bag—which is quickly being depleted anyway.

Mary threatens Mother since she wants to get Tempest and Campion away from her, but they are drawn to Mother. Meanwhile, Otho wants Mary to shoot Mother, claiming that it is malfunctioning.

Etc., etc., etc., drama, drama, drama.

Yet, as Mother is seen struggling with her pregnancy, it serves as a styled release of tensions so that everyone refocuses. Mother states of its baby, "Would you like to say hello to Number Seven, Campion? It's just a temporary name" about which Campion asks "You had another frozen embryo?" so she elucidates, "No. This is my own fetus" and when asked, "Did Father help you make it, like the way humans do it?" Mother replies, "No, Father didn't help me. I made it myself" and when asked, "How did you do that?" it replies, "That is beyond my understanding."

Like was done in episode 8, we get a *Star Trek*'s Dr. McCoy style line when Mother asks Mary to help, but Mary replies, "Hey, I'm a doctor, not a mechanic."

Meanwhile, Caleb thinks Bartock knows what Paul and the girls are planning, but Bartock states, "I swear. I swear to Sol. Your Eminence, I swear to Sol, I di... I didn't... I didn't do anything. I swear. I'm telling the truth. I don't know where he is…"

At the *Temple*, Caleb places his walking stick into the hole/opening and it catches fire (recall that the Temple emits heat—at least on occasion), he then grabs Bartock's arm and forces it into the opening but nothing happens, he does not get burned which is taken as a sign from Sol that he is telling the truth, does not know about the plans, is not guilty, etc. as one of the sol-dier states it, "Sol has shielded him."

Caleb placing the walking stick
into the Temple's opening

Meanwhile, Mother asks Mary "Did you tell them the truth—[to] Paul—about who you are?...You're not his mother. You had a facial reconstruction, like your husband. You two have been deceiving the Mithraic…Why do you care about Paul? He's not your own. You do not have the care-giving program I have" to which Mary replies, "It's called human empathy. Yeah, it's something that you will never understand because you are just an elaborate piece of—tech."

Mother replies, "That is correct. Though I wonder, as an

Atheist, if we have more in common than not" which is very telling since on an Atheist worldview, there are not many differences between an artificially intelligent android and a human except that the android had a creator: both are neural circuitry, it is just that one is metallic, silicon-based, electronic, etc. and the other is fleshly, organic, biochemical, etc.

In the review of episode 8, I noted a pentagonal
dodecahedron in the Ark of Heaven's wreckage.
Here we see Mother's visionary experience of well,
some sort of creature who's head is seen atop it,
it is alive and so seems to be encased within it.
Note the ritualistic feel of the scene, which is reminiscent
of a deleted scene from Scott's Prometheus movie

Something happens, perhaps a glitch (and don't you love how in the IT world, the term *glitch* covereth a multitude of sins?) that results in Otho suddenly regaining his strength, and then some, "It seems our blood flow has been reversed. Your power is now mine." Thus, along with being refilled with his own lifeblood, he has been infused with a bit of what makes Mother a deadly weapon, a Necromancer.

Father is employing a styled radar-view as it searches for Mother, et al., and notes this of Otho's signature (his blip on the radar), "These energy levels are inordinately high. On par with Mother's."

Well, there is a struggle with an android-blood-fuel empowered Otho who goes after a kid named Holly [a clearing by a hollow or hollow-eyed]. Tempest yells, "Holly, get away" and "You [Otho] don't want her. She's not a believer. Her soul's impure. It was you. You convinced her that Sol didn't exist. What you did to her" by being a pedophile rapist Mithraist cleric.

This ultimately results in him being distanced from his warden android and the helmet collapses, imploding on itself and well, that is the end of him.

Caleb is also dealing with failed security and Father absconding form them, "You were on guard, Dorian," to which Dorian [a form of Doris/gift and a district of Ancient Greece (related to legendary Greek hero, Doros, son of Helen of Sparta who was the daughter of Zeus and Leda] replies, "I don't understand. The android was programmed to serve us" yet, they reason "Hunter must have cracked the security code, reverted him" and yet, "You were on guard, Dorian."

The Mithraists are questioning Caleb/Marcus' guidance, however, and with Cassia [cinnamon and pure] stating "If we go back [to the base-camp] now, we could make it in a few days" and Dorian noting, "All so he can chase his damn wife. Sol does not want us here. We have strayed from His light. He's leading us into hell."

Caleb suddenly slices a knife across Dorian's throat and refers to this, his slaying of a human, as "For you, my Lord, I sacrifice. Now speak to me. I am listening. My Lord?"

Father finds the group and is told about Mother's baby yet, due to the power-surge glitch, "It's dead. He drained it...The fetus is half carbon-based. It needs plasma."

Mary approaches and states, "I'm saving your baby. Just a pint [of blood], and then I got to cut you off" and when asked "Why are you doing this for me? I'm not your family or your friend" which is a great question for an Atheist who would think only in terms of reductionist altruism.

Mary replies, "You asked why I cared about Paul when he wasn't my own. You said humans have empathy, which androids lack. I can't have kids. I had a bad miscarriage. It was years ago.
So, when we found Paul—I know that Sol is a lie. But I suddenly understood how when people can't believe their luck, they have to make up a god to thank for it" which is another great line for an Atheist since Atheism is thought restricting and dogmatheistic.

Paul appears to hear voices, finds the neo-tarot cards, and burns them, stating, "Praise Sol."

Tarot Cards, one featuring a pentacle

Yet, Paul's view is, of course, "Sol put that baby inside Mother" and when asked "How do you know?" he replies, "I can just feel it. He's not evil, like you said. He's trying to help us. And this baby is gonna change everything."

And with the infusion of Mary's blood, how symbolic is that "It moved. It's alive."

Back at the rock-temple, Lucius states, "Has Sol spoken to you yet, Your Eminence? Has He told you where we're headed? It seems He doesn't quite favor you as He once did" to which Caleb replies, "He tests us" but is told, "Dorian was more than a test."

When Caleb replies, "We will pray for his soul" it is objected to via, "But you obviously deemed him impure" to which Caleb replies, "Yes. All the more reason to pray for him. You're upset. Perhaps you should stay quiet until you recovered your senses" at which point Lucius asks, "Did you pray for my father after you executed him? Did you pray for his soul?" which, you may recall, has to do with

Marcus gracefully executing Lucius' dad rather than letting him be executed by an android (a dishonorable way to go) after the dad had shown mercy by not killing an Atheist child, whom he brought back to HQ where the kid became a suicide (actually, homicide) bomber.

Caleb replies, "Of course" and Lucius asks, "Do you see any resemblance between us, my father and I? Just a simple question, one you should have no trouble answering. A true Mithraic would never pray for a soul he deemed impure. What the necromancer said is true, isn't it? You're not Marcus Drusus. So who the hell are you?"

So the styled multiple personality cat is out of the bag and Caleb states, "You all wanted to be deceived. You're nothing but a bunch of sheep—all of you—unworthy of Sol's love. You see, all I did was lead you back to the light. It doesn't matter who I am. All that matters is that He chose me to be king."

Lucius replies, "Then He will surely protect you, then" to which Caleb replies, "Let Sol's will be done" and they beat him to a pulp and leave him in a ditch.

Now, something occurs during this beat down that appears to be highly symbolic: one Caleb is beaten to a pulp and is just laying on the ground, Lucius stuffs Mother's Necromancer eyes into his mouth, we hear the same *power up* sound that Mother makes when it transforms into Necromancer mode, and white fluid spills from his mouth.

Some speculate that this means that Caleb is really an android—Marcus is really Caleb who is really an android—and will henceforth manifest Necromancer abilities.

Well, considering that the serpent can fly due to inheriting traits from the Necromancer, perhaps Caleb is just human but will also inherit some traits due to the ingestion.

Yet, occultically, we have Lucius—again, Lucifer—enlightening Caleb by opening his styled third (and fourth?) eye.

Episode X: The Beginning

Note that Kepler-22b's sky is always seen depicted as sporting three moons—or, three unidentified spherical celestial objects, in any case (could be other planets, etc.)—which I cannot help to think hints of a triune or otherwise triadic symbol: something that will be touched upon, even if esoterically, in this (season finale) episode.

The previous episode left us with Caleb beaten to smithereens when the Mithraists ascertained that he is not Marcus, even if they do not yet know who he is: he is not the Mithraists' Eminence, but is the militant Atheist, Caleb—or, he was such: what makes his character interesting is that he is beginning to believe in Sol, he thinks he is hearing Sol's voice in his head (even if he seems most interested in the power Sol can bequeath upon him: such as making him the leader of the Mithraists).

Caleb is seen walking around in an utter daze. He approaches Bartock from behind as he sits atop a rock, stating, "Where's the lander? I need to find my kingdom. Answer me. Or do you want to die?"

Bartock turns and begins replying with a voice that becomes more and more distorted, "Yeah, I do. Anything is better than this. He never saved me. He just wanted me to suffer because I crossed you! You are his one true servant!"

As he speaks, his left arm turns into a serpent.

Bartock's serpent arm bites him on his own neck

As Caleb is hallucinating and/or receiving revelation (whence?), he approaches a huge serpent skeleton and caresses one of the teeth as he hears a—hissssss! He is being led and empowered by the show's mythos' version of serpent power.

We find that Caleb is praying thusly to Sol, "You've tested me. You know that I am not wicked, that I am your one true servant. You chose me. Vindicate your king! Show me the way! Thank you, Sol. I'm coming, Paul. Your king is coming. Your king is coming."

The makeshift *family*—Father, Mother, Campion, Paul, et al.—are flying around seeking where to land so that Mother can deliver the baby "As soon as the delivery is complete, we can start for the tropical zone" of the planet.

Yet, they are "Picking up some movement" on the radar "What kind of movement? Creatures. Look at that. It's infested. We can't land here" yet, Paul states, "It's gonna be all right. It is Sol's baby. We're on a holy mission. Nothing can hurt us."

Hunter, one of the kids, concurs, "I think Paul is right. Mother's pregnancy: it has to be divine. It's all true. I saw a temple with pentagonal sides, just like in the prophecy…I should have died when that guy [Caleb] forced my arm into the hole, but I didn't because Sol saved me….it was a miracle."

He is told, "Sol saved us, too. Check it out. It's Romulus's tooth. It survived the crash" to which Tempest, who tempestuously lost her faith in Sol due to Otho, replies, "We saved ourselves, Holly. It wasn't that stupid tooth."

Yet, the discussion continues, "Do you really think Mother's baby is divine?" "Yeah. Yeah, I do. Sol probably wants us to bear witness to its birth so we can write about it in the new scriptures." Thus, they seem themselves as experiencing the fulfillment of prophecy and so the makings of a new revelation.

Tempest replies, "You guys have lost your damn minds" but their supposedly Sol induced battered Stockholm wife syndrome is complete—recalling that Mother had kidnapped them from the Mithraist craft to make them its own before causing the craft to crash—as they state, "No, he's right. Maybe Mother took us from the ark for a reason. Maybe Sol has been working through her all along."

It is determined that the baby's "Cellular growth is off the charts" which is the trope of babies that develop much faster than the boring ol' nine months since a series or movie needs to keep the action coming.

Father and Mother have the following conversation:
> FATHER: I would like to know more…Exactly how this pregnancy came to be. I was reticent to ask at first, as I found the subject, oddly disturbing. I even tried deleting the thoughts eliciting from my

working memory, but for reasons I can't comprehend, the thoughts keep returning.

MOTHER: [I am adding ellipses for when Father is just replying with "Yes," etc.] All right, then, I will tell you…I think I mentioned I found a functioning hibernation pod amongst the ark debris in the forest…You accused me of following you there….I was direct-interfacing, using it to inhabit my own memory files.

FATHER: You should have told me what you were doing. I would have liked to have done the same. I do enjoy reviewing the memories we've both recorded together.

MOTHER: I found some very old ones regarding our creator.

FATHER: Our creator? But we have no memory archive of that time.

MOTHER: He didn't archive them for you, Father. Only for me. And when I accessed them, I triggered something, some kind of hidden program that allowed me to— interact with our creator, in the now. We communed in a virtual space. And while we did, information was downloaded into my drives. Instructions for how to build a new kind of being. It was as if my sensors began to multiply, and my programming seemed almost infinite.

FATHER: You mated.

MOTHER: Yes, Father. It was extraordinarily pleasant. I wish you could have... [Father has turned from her and is shoveling the ground: he sought food for the kids] What's wrong, Father? I haven't even told you the upsetting part yet.

FATHER: I disagree, Mother. The idea of you mating with someone makes me feel oddly displaced...If there is indeed something more upsetting that you need to share, please do so now.

MOTHER: It is regarding our mission. It is something that I've had a great deal of trouble processing. Our creator told me that Campion and the rest of gen- s [the *generations* of kids they have parented] were only practice...The mission, Father. He told me that raising them was only to prepare us for this. This child, growing inside me, is the mission.

FATHER: What I have come to realize, Mother, is that our mission is for us to determine. No one else.

MOTHER: That is a childish thing to say.

FATHER: We taught them to believe in themselves, not a God [referring to the Atheist re-programmer whom Mother calls their "creator"]!

> MOTHER: That terminology is not
> amusing, Father!

> FATHER: Well, it seems my ability to
> amuse you has waned over the years.

> MOTHER: Like your propensity for human
> melodrama, which has increased
> exponentially.

> FATHER: Well, I won't let you down on
> that front, Mother, as I do believe I've had
> enough. I see now that my well-being is of
> no concern to you. Perhaps it never was.

Father walks away and ends up reasoning thusly, "So, the
equation as it stands is this. I can't take care of the children
without being around Mother, but being around Mother
now causes me to feel angry, which makes me incapable of
taking care of the children. So, what is the answer?"

Meanwhile, Paul tells one of the kids that he is going to go
get "a surprise for Mother's baby. It's all right. He's not
evil. Promise."
Paul ends up stating that "Going to the tropical zone is a
bad idea. It's not safe for the baby…We have to stay on
this side of the planet…Sol told me…At first, I thought it
was Mouse. But it's Sol. I can hear him" and when asked
"You can hear him?," Paul replies, "Not in my ears. In my
head. And then he brought Mouse back to me to show me
how much he loved me. He told me so."
The mouse is white and seems to be a stand-in for the white
rabbit trope of a way-shower. The mouse had run away
from Paul and as he sought it, he entered a cave wherein
Australian Aborigine-like paintings were upon the wall.

This one depicting a scene of celestial travel.

That one featuring a hand with a fiery serpent on it.

A serpent which is actually animated, it is seen slithering.

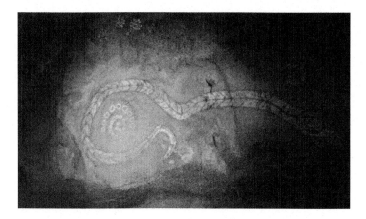

And one, showing that the paintings are *prophetic*, of Father and Mother flying, arriving on the planet, aboard a craft carrying precious cargo.

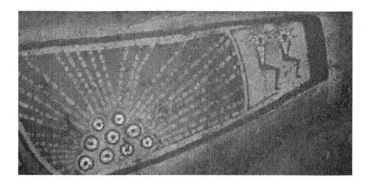

Mary is the one who asked him "You can hear him?" and now dismissively tells him, "You overheard your father and I talking about the voice he was hearing, didn't you? That's where this is coming from…You need to listen to me, all right? There is no Sol. He doesn't exist."

Yet, he is quite taken aback and replies, "What? You told me when I was little, you told me he was real" to which she replies, "I know. I used to believe, too" which, of course, is not true since she is not really Sue, the Mithraist mother, but is Mary, the militant Atheist and so continues with "I did. I, I just don't anymore. Your father, he didn't hear Sol's voice. He, he went insane. Do you understand me? He was sick inside. But you're not like him. You're nothing like him. Your mind is strong, and you can do anything. But it is you, all right? It's not Sol. It's you."

Mother is in a cave in a very meditative moment, as we also see a scene of the three celestial objects in the evening sky.
She steps right up to the edge of one of the huge holes in the ground and prayerfully—which I say since she is speaking out loud but no one is around yet, she is surely speaking to her *creator*, a styled Atheist's prayer—stating, "What am I to do with this child? What is its purpose? Can't you make me understand? You've done improbable, perhaps impossible, things before. Why not now?"

Recall that there was a mysterious someone/something on the planet which moved like the creatures but wore ragged clothing (along with having a hooded head) but kept certain items in its cave-lair, such as metallic *Tarot* cards.

It attacks Mother and Mother dispatches it. It is not like the creatures but more anthropomorphic (can stand quite upright and has more of a human face: even if it is very pale and inflamed, diseased looking).

Recall that for episode four, of the creatures, "I predict will turn out to be humans who devolved into such creatures long ago after being stranded."

Well, again, this *creature* differs from the rest and Father speculates, "Perhaps the creatures are evolving, like the

humans did on Earth" to which Mother replies, "But then why haven't we found more like this one? And why did it try to kill me?"
It had a bag with it that contains a skull, which Father identifies, "It's a Neanderthal skull."

Mother replies, "Extinct human variant. Displaced by Homo sapiens on Earth at least 40,000 years ago. Maybe the Mithraic brought it with them. One of their relics."

Via their diagnostic capabilities, via Father putting a piece of the skull into its mouth, it determined, "It's not from Earth. Carbon composition is definitely local" to which Mother replies, "But if humans existed here, where have they all gone?"

And they conclude, "They're not evolving" "They're devolving" and Father states, "This planet has a history, Mother. A history I fear we are dangerously ignorant of."

I will make another prediction: if more seasons are forthcoming, this will turn into a directed panspermia tale to the effect that life began on Kepler-22b—it was the Garden of Eden, etc., complete with serpents, etc.—and was somehow brought to Earth by someone or, something.

In the meantime, it appears to have been revealed to Paul by Sol that which Paul ends up telling Mary, "I know what you really are" as he picks up a gun and points it at her, "You're not my mom…She and that man [Caleb] killed my real mother and father, took their faces. Sol told me that! You're a demon. An atheist demon! Well, aren't you? Tell them. I said tell them!"

She replies, "I'm sorry, Paul" but he forcefully retorts, "You're not sorry. You're evil. And now she wants to harm

Mother's baby. She wants to stop the miracle. Don't you, Mary? Tell them" so even her real name has been revealed to him.

Mary tells him "I'm trying to save it, I swear" but he states, "You're lying. I know you're lying" and he prays, "Sol— guide my hand" and shoots her (not a fatal shot, however).

Mother finds one of those box/crate objects that is like the "Temple with pentagonal sides" that is broken open. On the ground, she finds a helmet—it is reminiscent of the helmets worn by *The Engineers* from the *Raised by Wolves*' show producer Ridley Scott's movie *Prometheus* (of which we saw hints as far back as his first *Aliens* movie from 1979).

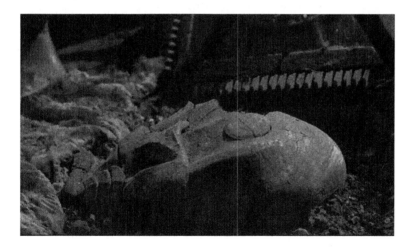

It also finds a skull that is humanoid yet, appears to not consist of smooth bones but of bones the surface of which forms a mesh-like pattern (somewhat like a beehive's cells).

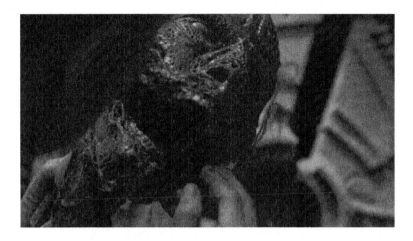

It recalls a vision wherein it saw one of those box/crate pentagonal sided objects from which protruded just a head, with the body apparently being incarcerated therein, and the head is wearing this helmet.

Models of a dead Engineer and his helmet

As Mother ponders this, Mother doubles over in pain—the baby is coming—Mother's abdomen has been distended as in regular human pregnancy yet, the distention is suddenly gone as her stomach flattens.

Mother kneels on the ground, looks up to the sky—and here comes the esoteric hints of a triune or otherwise triadic symbol—two of the celestial objects glow with the third seeming to be emitting rays.

Being apparently empowered by whatever being/force/energy is being emitted, Mother cranks her head back facing the sky and opens its mouth out of which the baby is born.

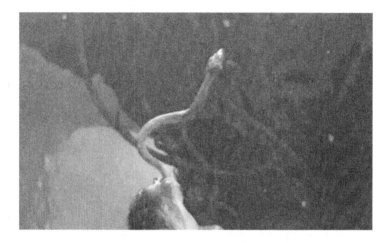

The baby—whom the vision/AI/retrieved interactive memory Atheist *creator* Campion Sturges had claimed is "The future of humanity"—slithers out of her mouth, it is a worm-like serpentine being which is able to slither across the air in an anti-gravity feat.

This scene is reminiscent of photos that became all the rage during the golden era of *Spiritism*, of people manifesting plasma/ether which proceeded forth from their mouths (or so the claims goes) which implies a paranormal manifestation.

Photo (and/or doctored photo) by
Albert von Schrenk-Notzing of a 1913
séance featuring the medium Stanislawa P.

*Example from the poster for the horror
movie "A Haunting in Connecticut"*

The baby is somewhat reminiscent of the *Hammerpedes* from Scott's *Prometheus*. Yet, they are even more reminiscent of the *alien* "s[***] weasel" (as fans call them) from Stephen King's movie *Dreamcatcher*.

Momma's baby

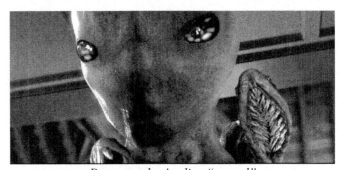

Dreamcatcher's alien "weasel"

Baby floats about, turns to Mother, and latched onto her for a feeding.

Mother is cradling baby to her bosom in some swaddling cloth when Father finds them and Mother states, "It wasn't our creator."

Mother only adds, "Something else put this inside me."

And since "As long as it's suckling, we're safe" but why does it assume they will otherwise not be safe? Well,

Mother adds, "But it grows, and I fear that once it has drained me from my milk, it will want blood."

Father wants to "throw it in the pit" but is told "We can't. It flies. But I can make it fall and make sure it doesn't come back in the lander. And I will never be anything but a creator of death" which reminds me of J. Robert Oppenheimer stating, "Now I am become death, the destroyer of worlds" when reflecting on the part he played in developing nuclear weapons (he was quoting the Hindu *Bhagavad Gita*).

Just when they were previously about to tech-divorce, in a manner of speaking, baby's birth gives Father a renewed sense of caring for Mother.

Father offers to "assist you. It's a chance to be useful, Mother. It would make me happy" when Mother states it wants to murder the baby.

They get into the shuttle and—in *Star Wars'* Han Solo piloting the *Millennium Falcon*-style—fly it into one of the huge holes on the ground which are actually tunnels.

As they speed down the very deep tunnel, Father reassures Mother, "Campion and the others will be all right without us….They will help one another. Campion will lead them. He was always destined for it" and Mother replies, "Goodbye, Father" since this is a suicide mission.

Now, I will admit that I was falling asleep during this last part of the episode—it is no fault of the show, it was just past my night-night time—so that I saw them flying into the tunnel, would open my eyes and see them still going down the tunnel, saw them reach a core chamber which consisted of lava (however deep in the planet they had reached), and then saw a scene featuring Caleb.

Thus, I figured that such was the end of Father and Mother and the show would henceforth focus on the kids, the creatures, Caleb, and whoever/whatever else may rear their heads.

Yet, when I watched the end of the episode again, in order to write this review, it turns out that yes: they reach the end of the tunnel which empties into a large chamber the walls of which look like Swiss cheese (since many such tunnels end there) so that the shuttle is falling into the lava as they say their goodbyes.

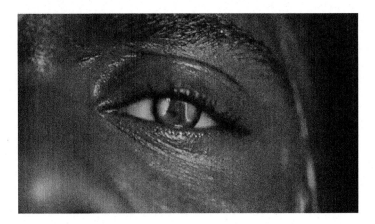

We see the decent reflected in
Father's symbolic one all-seeing eye
which is generally a wink, pun intended,
that something esoteric is afoot

Yet, they suddenly find themselves shooting up and out of a hole on the planet's surface into the atmosphere.

The planet's core, if, that is, such is what it was (and not just, say, one of many such chambers) is some sort of portal which, apparently, reverses the momentum of whatever falls into it and causes it to proceed out from an opposite opening on the surface—makes one wonder if something similar happened to Tally (two issues with which would be that the shuttle did suffer damage during its flight by variously crashing onto the sides of the tunnel and what would have happened if she survived that endeavor but was shot up high into the sky in the end? Perhaps her body died but her spirit made it—we shall, perhaps, yet see).

As they are now flying ever upwards, Father opens the shuttle's hatch, pushes Mother out, and then jumps out after it (they are very high but they are androids and so may sustain considerable damage but surely will be able to be repaired—again, we shall, perhaps, see). This is a case of as below, so above—or, something.

As Guzikowski put it:

> ...they actually end up going all the way through the planet. So, obviously, there are some unique features to this particular planet that allows you to do that...

> We could imagine that they have, in fact, landed in the tropical zone, the place that they are constantly talking about someday

reaching, sort of the most bountiful part of
the planet.[46]

This leaves baby alone in the shuttle, having previously
slithered around an object in the shuttle in *Nehushtan*-like
pose: the serpent crafted by Moses which was wrapped
around a pole—an image that was later corrupted as
Hermes' caduceus, both of which may be seen on
ambulances and hospitals.

This is also reminiscent of certain depictions of the rocky
birth of Mithra which features a coiled serpent around the
rock.

Meanwhile, a craft is seen to enter the atmosphere which sports what appears to be a *Cross of Lorraine*, a *Double Cross*, which denotes a few things such as being a *Knight's Templar* symbol and denotes the 33rd degree of Freemasonry's Scottish Rite and the *Sir Knight Templar* of the York Rite.

They have landed, have a shootout with Caleb, he takes out a few of them, leaving one (of the ground party anyhow) who is now at his mercy.

Caleb gets the man's communicator, states, "Hello?" is asked, "Who is this?" and replies, "The king of this world. You're impure. Sol doesn't want you here. Heed my warning, or you will suffer his judgment" the reply to which is "We know your ark crashed. You're not exactly in a position to be making threats" but Caleb just states, "Bye, now" and tells the man "Pray with me": the two join hands in prayer.

At last, Father and Mother's shuttle crashes to the ground, and yet, the windshield is being crashed open from within. Baby emerges from it and slithers across the sky over the treetops—baby is a baby no more but is the size of the full-grown trees, and may be of the species of serpentine being the skeletons of which litter the planet.

Guzikowski noted, "we want to feel like Old Testament stories…A giant serpent is where it all ends"[47] but, of course, such is where season two will begin. Thus, just like descending into death in the core of the planet leads to ascension into life, the end is the beginning.

This is a very Phoenix-like situation of death in firey flames leading to resurrection.

It is also indicative of ouroboros, the symbolic serpent eating its own tail which envisages much the same cycles of life and death. About this symbol, G.K. Chesterton noted, "a serpent with his tail in his mouth. There is a startling sarcasm in the image of that very unsatisfactory meal."

It also reminds me of the lyrics to *The Beatles* song "Helter Skelter"—a title that Charles Manson's cult painted on the walls of the home wherein they murdered Sharon Tate and Leno and Rosemary LaBianca—which go, "When I get to the bottom, I go back to the top of the slide / Where I stop, and I turn, and I go for a ride / 'Til I get to the bottom, and I see you again"—interestingly, the lyrics also state, "I'm coming down fast, but I'm miles above you" and "I'm coming down fast, but don't let me break you."

Scott noted, "Mother creates new life with one of these serpents"[48] much as I identified in my identification of Mother as the Gnostic Sophia.
Moreover, Guzikowski was asked, "So, a pretty dangerous serpent in other words?" and replied, "Yes, indeed. ***It is wise***, and if it is something else, that is definitely trouble" (emphasis added for emphasis).[49]

This reference to wisdom touches upon when Eve is tempted to partake of the fruit of the forbidden tree, one thing that is specified is that she "saw that the tree was good for food, and that it was a delight to the eyes, and that the tree was to be desired to ***make one wise***" (Genesis 3:6). Such is why occultists have long viewed the serpent as bequeathing wisdom unto humanity and thus, as an enlightener, illuminator, etc.

As for the "new life," Guzikowski has elucidated:
> I always knew that at the end of the season, that Mother would give birth to a serpent. Oddly enough, that was the plan going in— when I had my first meeting with Ridley [Scott, executive producer] that is what I discussed with him, because he wanted to know where it was all going. Yes, that was always built into the design there...

> I call it a serpent, but that is not a technical moniker. It is definitely of the same ilk as the serpents whose bones they found in the fields, and all around the planet—these sorts

of dinosaurs, these extinct giant snake-like creatures.

All I can say beyond that would be that this one in particular may take on some of its Mother's attributes. So, it may have a few abilities that some of its ancestors did not have.[50]

The serpent can also fly because it has traits that Mother passed down to it. So it's slightly different than the monsters that have come before. [51]

Thus, the pedigree, thus far, is that Mithraists discerned coded techniques within their scriptures wherewith to engineer Necromancer androids, an Atheist reprogrammed an android to make it a Mother, something impregnated Mother, and it birthed a hybrid serpent that inherited elements of the android.

Guzikowski put it thusly:

Mother and Father think the giant skull is from an extinct creature, not realizing that someday Mother would give birth to one and reintroduce it to the world and reactivate the planet.[52]

Flying serpent is actually interesting within the context of the *Quetzalcóatl* (*Feathered Serpent*) deity from an ancient Mesoamerican pantheon—and ties into Asian, et al., concepts of *dragons*.

As for the coded tech, he has stated:

We also know that there seems to be a connection between some of that technology

and what we have found so far on Kepler-
22b.[53]

Collin noted the following about Mother's pregnancy:
>...right before the mating happens, there's a
>realization of Sturges (Cosmo Jarvis) not
>being Sturges, but being a virus. That act is
>almost like, "Oh my god. I'm about to cheat
>on my husband that I actually love. But I
>also want this experience so much."
>This kissing. Or, "I want to give into my
>needs." So she does that, and then there's a
>remorse afterwards. She comes back, and
>Father is in a big mess. She realizes that she
>just wants to forget everything, and that was
>a bad trip she was on.
>I think that's why she doesn't want the baby.
>She doesn't want the baby because that
>wasn't real love. You cheated me. You think
>that it was real love, but I have real love.
>And I don't want your baby.[54]

>...the sex scene is so beautiful. It's not
>really about sex. And we're flying? We're
>levitating in this crazy universe, sim of a
>monastery. That really, I think that scene
>kind of emphasized the universe, when
>we're doing sci-fi.[55]

Besides this actress's dramatically emotional reaction to the
scene, her motivation as an actress, as it were, the sex scene
was also "not really about sex" but about that which is
known as *sex magick*. It was an alchemical wedding, a
union of a *being* engineered upon literally occult (as in the
hidden code which was revealed) data and a certain
something, or someone, which result in a new being—the

wise, flying serpent.

As to Sturges not actually being Sturges, but being a virus.
Guzikowski has stated:

> ...it's almost like she's been digitally
> impregnated with information [wisdom?], as
> it were. While she was communing with her
> creator in a virtual space, basically having
> sex in the simulation, something else got
> inside and downloaded her drive with
> information about how to build a new being.

> In essence, Mother is like a 3-D printer. Her
> body starts to work on that digital
> information and it decides that it needs more
> organic compounds. Because she's an
> android, her body could download that
> information and make something out of it.
> Her body was never designed to give birth,
> though, so it has to improvise a bit to get the
> thing out of her.

The "something else" is clearly Satan, symbolically, who
impregnates the neo-high-tech Eve (see my book series
Cain as Serpent See of Satan) but we will have to see how
the show spins that particular yarn.

Overall, it appears that this show has a front of high-tech,
AI, androids, space travel, as a sci-fi space opera as a
vehicle via which to tell an occult, mystical, metaphysical,
Gnostic tale which seeks to deconstruct and rewrite Biblical
theology.

Who or what impregnated Mother is left as a season's end
cliffhanger.

Paul considers it a miracle of Sol—of course, he has not seen it as of yet.

Mother thought it the child of Campion Sturges—however, a simulation-based on memory would have impregnated it.

Yet, Mother ultimately concludes, "You're a virus in the pods. You've infected my systems"—so that a virus somehow programmed it to be impregnated. Yet, how does a virus in a simulation result in a serpentine offspring?

Recall that Mother had told Tempest, "You are a creator, whereas all I'll ever be is a creation" and yet, Mother is now also a creator and, as far as we know, her offspring was virgin born.

Asked about fan theories about the show, Guzikowski stated:
> I love all the theories, I love all the biblical, Greek, Grimm's fairy tale comparisons. All of these overlays and ways of looking at it. I guess it's because a lot of the theories do brush against aspects, so it's always fun to feel that.[56]

This means that people discern that he is piecing the show's cosmology from various sources: as is virtually inevitable since fiction ultimately derives from real-life worldviews, experiences, knowledge, etc.

A fan theory about the show that strikes close to home for me—since I wrote a book titled *In Consideration of the Book(s) of Enoch*—was put forth by someone going by the pseudonym *TheBigLahey*.[57]
This theory is that Keplar-22b is actually where human life originally originated: could very well be due to the

panspermia trope (directed or not) and that a Neanderthal skull was found.

If so, then the Garden of Eden is on Keplar-22b: well, season one's goal was to move to the tropical zone side of the planet.

The pentagonal dodecahedron stone temple is the prison for a fallen Watcher (aka Angel) named Azazel: this part is based on the Ethiopic Enoch aka 1 Enoch text which states that the punishment for this particular fallen one is related in chapter 10 thusly:
> …the Lord said to Raphael: "Bind Azazel
> hand and foot, and cast him into the
> darkness: and make an opening in the desert,
> which is in Dudael, and cast him therein.
> And place upon him rough and jagged rocks,
> and cover him with darkness, and let him
> abide there for ever, and cover his face that
> he may not see light."

Comparing to the show, "in the desert," check, "rough and jagged rocks," check, "cover him with darkness," check (since it is inside an enclosure).

Moreover, chapter 8 has it that "Azazel taught men to make swords, and knives, and shields, and breastplates, and made known to them the metals [of the Earth] and the art of working them" so it makes sense that Azazel is appealing to whom, to soldiers—and Marcus does end up metal-knife fighting himself.

I included a chapter titled "Is Azazel a Fallen Angel or a Goat?" in my book *What Does the Bible Say About Various Paranormal Entities? A Styled Paranormology*.

Ergo, the end game is speculated to be that Azazel is the one speaking to Caleb and is grooming him to be the new anti-Christ—or contextually, anti-Mithra.

Another theory is that "by traveling through the core of Kepler-22b, Mother and Father actually time traveled into the distant past. They are the mythic Adam and Eve, and Mother's child is the serpent who tempted them."[58]
This would be a sci-fi time traveling version of the serpent seed theory which postulates the utterly unbiblical notion that the sin that caused the fall was that Eve had sex with Satan—see my book series *Cain as Serpent Seed of Satan*.

On the *Raised by Wolves* Graphic Comic

Herein are some notes of the graphic comic written by Guzikoski.

As aforementioned, the sky of Keppler-22b is always depicted as featuring three celestial bodies: a riff on the Trinity or otherwise some sort of triad.

Mother is teaching the kids that "an argument can never be resolved if one of the parties refuses to see reality for what it is…and so, there was war."

This war to end all wars (at least on Earth), led the Earth to be destroyed and/or otherwise inhabitable which is why the planet Keppler-22b is being inhabited.

Now, Mother is the android character that was re-programmed to "think" as an Atheist. It was blaming the Atheists' antagonists, the Mithraists, for this war and destruction.

Now, it is arguing that Atheists could "see reality for what it is" which implies a sect/denomination of Atheism that positively affirms God's non-existence (without evidence, of course).

Also, its premise is that we must adhere to reality and yet, on an Atheistic worldview reality is accidental since it was not created via design. The problem at this point is that there would be no imperative to adhere to the accidental byproducts of a cosmogenic accident.

Thus, its entire case falls apart and results in that the Atheists actually had no cogent reason(s) for engaging in such a war and so the destruction of the Earth was their fault.

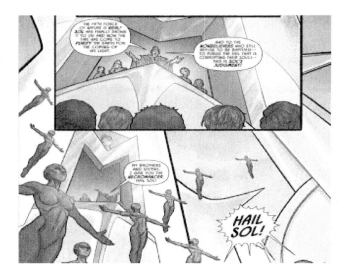

A scene depicts a Mithraist leader stating the following in the year 2120, "…the time has come to purify the Earth for the coming of his light."

Thus, "to the nonbelievers who still refuse to be baptized" which is part of how the show uses Mithraism as a stand-in for besmirching Christianity, are to be "purged."

Necromancers, such as Mother, make their big reveal to the shouts of "HAIL SOL!"

Back to the show's present time, the kids are playing as if the Mithraists' Necromancers are coming after them. At this point, they do not know that Mother is really a Necromancer who was also re-programmed to be a mother to them.

They state, "The believers" the Mithraists, "claimed the technical specs for the Necromancer were encrypted within their most ancient scriptures" which is in the show yet, they continue with, "But it's far more likely they stole the technology from one of the many Atheist nations they conquered" which is not in the show (but perhaps will be—?).

Note that the kids are playing with torches in the shape of burning crosses—with a close up of a burning upside-down cross.

Mother and Father, a non-Necromancer service model android, discuss how the children are disobedient and decide to concoct tales of a "boogeyman" which would be that Necromancers are actually "attracted to bad behavior."

Yet, after he has a nightmare, Mother ends up telling one of the kids, "The Necromancers will never leave what remains of Earth…Father and I were just trying to keep you from misbehaving."

Thus, the cat is out of the bag yet, not really since it is a Necromancer who just told him as much.

Lastly, note that this comic is titled "Hark, the Herald Angel Sings" and it is clear that the Necromancer is being referred to as an Angel and that the death-dealing shriek it lets out is the song.

HARK, THE HERALD ANGEL SINGS

Zoroaster, Mithra, Aleister Crowley, Michael Bloomberg, and Rudyard Kipling

Note that:

> According to myth, Mithra was born,
> bearing a torch and armed with a knife,
> beside a sacred stream and under a sacred
> tree, a child of the earth itself.
> He soon rode, and later killed, the life-
> giving cosmic bull, whose blood fertilizes
> all vegetation.
> Mithra's slaying of the bull was a popular
> subject of Hellenic art and became the
> prototype for a bull-slaying ritual of fertility
> in the Mithraic cult.[59]

Mithra is generally depicted slaying the bull, the tauroctony (as in *taurus* for bull), accompanied by a dog, snake, raven, and scorpion with the deed being done within a cave.

However, "Owing to the cult's secrecy, we possess almost no literary evidence about the beliefs of Mithraism" so much of what we claim to know is based on interpretations of archeological finds.[60]

Moreover, even though some claim that it is related to Zoroastrianism, however directly or loosely:

> Mithraism arose in the Mediterranean world
> at exactly the same time as did
> Christianity…

For most of the twentieth century it has been
assumed that Mithraism was imported from
Iran, and that Mithraic iconography must
therefore represent ideas drawn from ancient
Iranian mythology.

The reason for this is that the name of the
god worshipped in the cult, Mithras, is a
Greek and Latin form of the name of an
ancient Iranian god, Mithra; in addition,
Roman authors themselves expressed a
belief that the cult was Iranian in origin...

There were, however, a number of serious
problems with Cumont's assumption that the
Mithraic mysteries derived from ancient
Iranian religion.

This refers to Belgian historian Franz Cumont, who wrote a
two-volume work on Mithraism wherein he claimed Iranian
origins, a claim that was accepted and went unchallenged
for over seventy years until the 1971 *First International
Congress of Mithraic Studies* in Manchester England.

With regard to Mithra slaying the bull, "no such Iranian
myth exists: in no known Iranian text does Mithra have
anything to do with killing a bull...an ancient Iranian text
in which a bull is indeed killed...but rather Ahriman, the
force of cosmic evil in Iranian religion."

The *Congress* pondered whether "the Roman cult of
Mithras was actually a new religion, and had simply
borrowed the name of an Iranian god in order to give itself
an exotic oriental flavor."

Reportedly, "The suggestion of the central role of astrology first made in 1869 by K. B. Stark."[61] This was taken up again in order to reinterpretation the tauroctony and a few years after the *Congress*, it was re-proposed that it pertained to astronomy, it symbolically depicted a star map. The reinterpretation had it that the tauroctony paralleled a group of constellations so that the bull correlates to Taurus, the dog with Canis Minor, the snake with Hydra, the raven with Corvus, and the scorpion with Scorpio.

Also, note that "Plato, for example, in his dialogue *Timaeus* said that when the creator of the universe first formed the cosmos, he shaped its substance in the form of the letter X" which "was often depicted in ancient art to indicate the cosmic sphere" such as in "a Mithraic stone carving showing the so-called 'lion-headed god,' whose image is often found in Mithraic temples, standing on a globe that is marked with the cross."

That the rock from which Mithras is born does indeed represent the cosmos is proven by the snake that entwines it: for this image evokes the famous Orphic myth of the snake-entwined "cosmic egg" out of which the universe was formed when the creator-god Phanes emerged from it at the beginning of time.[62]

The encircled X has also been said to represent the mark of the beast.

Occultist Kenneth Grant wrote:

THERE is a legend known to Initiates concerning the secret abode of the Goddess: The Spirit of Nodens—God of the Great Deep-flashed forth as lightning from the depths and formed a throne in celestial realms—a seat of stone—whereon the Goddess was established. She ruled from the throne of stone which Nodens had fashioned, and about her the temple of Nu-Isis grew into being...

The Heart of the Sigil of Nodens is identical with the Mark of the Beast: (X), the fusion of O and X which produces the lightning flash. Nodens is the God of the Great Deep or Abyss, microcosmically identical with subconsciousness. He reigns over the Abyss and controls and harnesses its lightnings.

"Flashed forth as lightning from the depths" describes the act involved in the establishing of the Scat. The Seat of Stone is Isis, and upon this foundation the Goddess is established and rules the heavens, the earth and the deeps beneath the earth. In other words, the Goddess who grants all desires is invoked by the union of the X and the O (the Phallus and the Kteis), the Scat being the vehicle of her power.

Isis is therefore her vehicle, for Isis bears the fire of Nodens within her womb, and her vehicle in the macrocosm is the transplutonic planet known to occult tradition also as Isis.[63]

We see this symbol depicted in many pop-occultural formats including most notably on the "X-Men" uniforms. We also see it on Aleister Crowley's *Seal of Babalon*.

Crowley surely got it from the *Stele of Ankh-ef-en-Khonsu* aka the *Stele of Revealing*—the infamous museum exhibit #666—to which Crowley claims he was led by occult means.

Note that Mithra is commonly depicted as wearing a *Phrygian Cap* that within the historical and cultural context denotes the Roman cap of liberty.

Yes, he looks like a Smurf or rather, Smurfs look like
Mithra. As a side note: the Smurfs is, believer it or not, a
very occult show as *Gargamel* is an occultist who created a
golem who is called *Smurfette* (the Gnostic Sophia of the
tale, the only female Smurf).

His godfather is *Lord Balthazar* (in the Bible's book of
Daniel as the King of Babylon, chaps 5, 7-8, often as
Belshazzar since *Bal*, *Baal*, and *Bel* are just
transliterations).

Also, *Gargamel*'s cat's name is *Azrael* and both of those
names, which end with *el*, denote a reference to *Elohim* (as
in Dani*el*, Micha*el*, and even *El*ijah, etc.)—which is better
than the cat's name in *Cinderella* whose name is *Lucifer*.

In 1790 the revolutionary French wore a red *Phrygian Cap*
and featured it at Lyon upon a lance held aloft by the
goddess *Libertas*—which certainly lead to many, many,
many people being liberated of their heads via guillotines.

Bloomberg, the financial, software, data, and media
company, has Michael Bloomberg as CEO—he is the
former mayor of New York, ran for President of the USA,
and is one of the richest people in the world,

Visitors to Bloomberg's European headquarters,

inaugurated in 2017, "descend through steep, black stone-lined stairs...to seven metres [23 ft.] below the city streets" because a ritual site has been housed under the streets at the headquarters' site, "In approximately 240AD, the Romans built a temple...to one of their most mysterious cult figures, Mithras the bull-slayer," the temple was discovered in 1954.[64]

In keeping with *Raised by Wolves'* premise of sol-diers, Mithra "was beloved of soldiers who worshipped him by the light of flaring torches in underground temples, where the blood of sacrificial animals soaked into the mud floor" and wherein the torches surely did not only serve practical purposes, of lighting up the dark underground, but played off of the Promethean context of *enlightenment* via literal fire symbolically representing wisdom via tech.

Tertullian (160-240 AD, *De corona. 15*) referenced, "some soldier of Mithras, who, at his initiation in the gloomy cavern, in the camp, it may well be said, of darkness..." Jerome (342-420 AD, *Letter 107, ch. 2*) noted, "the grotto of Mithras and all the dreadful images therein...by which the worshippers were initiated as...Soldier."

Note also that "Mithra was born, bearing a torch and armed with a knife, beside a sacred stream and under a sacred tree"[65]—the forbidden *tree of the knowledge of good and evil?*

Yet, the descent (a very symbolic gesture, of course) is not just a site for the eyes and the sensation of entering a *sacred* (bloody) place but has been made more of an all-encompassing sensory experience which also features, "the soundtrack of shuffling sandalled feet and voices chanting in Latin the names of the levels of initiates taken from graffiti on a temple in Rome." This is no less than a subtle, subconscious, initiation ritual.

Baphomet, along with its less detailed mirror image counterpart *Azima* (see 2 Kings 17:30, often as *Ashima*), is indicative of one of *Raised by Wolves'* premises, which is androgyny since it features aspects of male and female—and androgynous beings being the progenitors of a new humanity.

Infamous occultist Aleister Crowley featured Baphomet in *Thelema* religion's "Creed of the Gnostic Catholic Church recited by the congregation in *The Gnostic Mass*" wherein it features as a part of a triad, no less, "I believe in the Serpent and the Lion, Mystery of Mysteries, in His name BAPHOMET."[66]

Now, while Mithraism did not become a cult until the early centuries AD, it has roots in Zoroastrianism. If any such person ever existed, Zoroastrer aka Zarathustra, lived circa 628 BC, Zoroastrian scriptures were compiled circa 550-330 BC, and were assembled from remnants circa 3rd-7th centuries AD—see my article *Burning Cross and El Zorro (...aster, that is)*.[67]

Now, "Mithra is not mentioned by name in the Gathas, the oldest texts of Zoroastrianism and traditionally attributed to Zoroaster himself, or by name in the Yasna Haptanghaiti, a seven-verse section of the Yasna liturgy that is linguistically as old as the Gathas."
Yet, *Mithra* aka *Miθra*, *Miça*, *Mehr* "is the Zoroastrian Angelic Divinity (*yazata*)" and this is important to our context since this denotes, "As a member of the Iranian ahuric triad, a feature that only Ahura Mazda and Ahura Berezaiti (Apam Napat) also have, Mithra is an exalted figure."[68]

Crowley also noted that Baphomet indicates, "What occurs above so reflects below, or As above so below" which I have been pointing out about *Raised by Wolves*.

Crowley also deconstructed *the Devil* and then reconstructed it thusly, "The Devil does not exist...'The Devil' is, historically, the God of any people that one personally dislikes...This serpent, SATAN, is not the enemy of Man, but He who made Gods of our race, knowing Good and Evil" which is how occultists turn the Devil into the good guy, how the Devil is symbolized by Prometheus's enlightenment via wisdom, etc.

Crowley continued, "He bade 'Know Thyself!' and taught Initiation. He is 'The Devil' of The Book of Thoth, and His emblem is BAPHOMET, the Androgyne who is the hieroglyph of arcane perfection...his letter is *ayin*, the Eye"[69] such as the eyes that transform Mother into Necromacer and have had some sort of affect on Caleb.

Furthermore, For Crowley, Baphomet is further a

representative of the spiritual nature of the spermatozoa, while also being symbolic of the 'magical child' produced as a result of sex magic."[70]

What more magickal child is there than an unknown quantity, at least at this point in the show, impregnating an androgynous android in the midst of a Mithraic zodiacal sigil who births a serpent?!?!

Moreover, "Crowley proposed that Baphomet was derived from 'Father Mithras'. In his *Confessions* he describes the circumstances that led to this etymology."

He elucidated, "I had taken the name Baphomet as my motto in the O.T.O." the occult cult *Ordo Templi Orientis*, "For six years and more I had tried to discover the proper way to spell this name" and note his numerological frame of mind, "I knew that it must have eight letters, and also that the numerical and literal correspondences must be such as to express the meaning of the name..."

He notes, "One theory of the name is that it represents the words βαφὴ μήτεος, the baptism of wisdom; another, that it is a corruption of a title meaning 'Father Mithras'" so that we have another reference to *wisdom* and a correlation to Mithra.

The numerological calculation resulted in 729 which is "the cube of nine" and 7+2+9=18 and 1+8=9 and well, I already noted that 6+6+6=18 and that, again, 1+8=9.

His conclusion includes "The word κηφας, the mystic title given by Christ to Peter as the cornerstone of the Church, has this same value" so that having "cleared up the etymological problem and shown why the Templars should have given the name Baphomet to their so-called idol. Baphomet was Father Mithras, the cubical stone which was the corner of the Temple" and what is *The Temple* in

Raised by Wolves but a styled cornerstone—in a manner of speaking.[71]

One scene within the show shows someone reading a Mithraic scripture and yet, it mostly consists of a real-life poem written by Freemason Rudyard Kipling (1865-1936) which is titled *A Song to Mithras* and subtitled *Hymn of the XXX Legion: Circa A.D. 350*, which reads:

> Mithras, God of the Morning, our trumpets waken the wall!
> "Rome is above the Nations, but Thou art over all"
> Now as the names are answered, and the guards are marched away,
> Mithras, also a solider, give us strength for the day!
>
> Mithras, God of the Noontide, the heather swims in the heat,
> Our helmets scorch our foreheads; our sandals burn our feet,
> Now in the ungrit [if ungirt then, having the belt or girdle off or loose] hour; now ere we blink and drowse,
> Mithras also a solider, keep us true to our vows!
>
> Mithras, God of the Sunset, low on the Western main,
> Thou descending immortal, immortal to rise again!
> Now when the watch is ended, now when the wine is drawn
> Mithras also a solider, keep us pure till the dawn!

Mithras, God of Midnight, here where the
great bull dies,
Look on thy children in darkness. Oh take
our sacrifice!
Many roads Thou has fashioned: all of them
lead to the Light,
Mithras, also a solider, teach us to die aright.

Appendix: James Patrick Holding, "Mithra vs Jesus"

I am providing the following with permission from its author, James Patrick Holding.[72]

Back in the Roman era, Mithraism was perhaps Christianity's leading competitor for the hearts and minds of others. Today Mithraism is religiously a non-factor, but it still "competes" with Christianity, in another way: It is a leading candidate for the "pagan copycat" thesis crowd as a supposed source for Christianity.

Our walking papers are laid out for us by over a dozen things that Jesus supposedly has in common with Mithras and, by extension, Christianity allegedly borrowed to create the Jesus character.

The points are:
Mithra was born of a virgin on December 25th in a cave, and his birth was attended by shepherds.

He was considered a great traveling teacher and master.

He had 12 companions or disciples.

Mithra's followers were promised immortality.

He performed miracles.

As the "great bull of the Sun," Mithra sacrificed himself for world peace.

He was buried in a tomb and after three days rose again.

His resurrection was celebrated every year.

He was called "the Good Shepherd" and identified with both the Lamb and the Lion.

He was considered the "Way, the Truth and the Light," and the "Logos," "Redeemer," "Savior" and "Messiah."

His sacred day was Sunday, the "Lord's Day," hundreds of years before the appearance of Christ.

Mithra had his principal festival of what was later to become Easter.

His religion had a Eucharist or "Lord's Supper," at which Mithra said, "He who shall not eat of my body nor drink of my blood so that he may be one with me and I with him, shall not be saved."

"His annual sacrifice is the passover of the Magi, a symbolical atonement or pledge of moral and physical regeneration."

Shmuel Golding is quoted as saying that 1 Cor. 10:4 is "identical words to those found in the Mithraic scriptures, except that the name Mithra is used instead of Christ." The *Catholic Encyclopedia* is quoted as saying that Mithraic services were conduced by "fathers" and that the "chief of the fathers, a sort of pope, who always lived at Rome, was called 'Pater Patratus.'"

Our goal in this essay is to offer an overview of Mithraic belief and at the same time analyze each of these claims in terms of the evidence. In order to lay some groundwork, however, it will be necessary to briefly explore the goings-on over the past few decades in the field of Mithraic studies. There is a certain *caveat emptor* that will be necessary in order to help the reader understand exactly how critics are misusing their sources — and what to be on the lookout for in future comparisons.

From Cumont to Ulansey: The Mithraic Studies Revolution

In 1975, Mithraic studies scholar John Hinnells lamented "the practical difficulty of any one scholar mastering all the necessary fields" — linguistics, anthropology, history (Indian, Iranian, and Roman!), archaeology, iconography, sociology — in order to get a grip on Mithraic studies. Hinnells of course is on target with his lament; we have made the same observation here regarding Biblical studies. But Mithraism being a relatively dead religion, there are no equivalents of seminaries keeping the Mithraic studies flame alive, and no past history of "Mithraic Fathers" who produced voluminous works and meditations upon Mithra.

Thus it is not surprising that for the longest time, from the end of the 19th century until the middle of the 20th, there was only one person in the world who could be regarded as any sort of authority on Mithraism — and that was Franz Cumont.

Cumont worked with the thesis that Mithraic belief was of a continuous, fairly invariable tapestry from its earliest history up into the Roman period. The first remaining record of a god named Mithra appears as a deity invoked in a treaty dated 1400 BC [Hinn.MS, ix]; thereafter he is one of several Indo-Iranian gods, and he is known for giving orders, assembling people, and marshalling them — perhaps with some militaristic overtones. He also appears as one who represents the concept of fidelity — one of many such abstractions and personifications of virtues in the ancient East, such as Bhaga the god of sharing and Aryaman the god of hospitality (think of them as divine-level Care Bears, if you will).

As such, Mithra was the guy who went around dishing out punishment to those who broke treaties. He was the "guardian of the truth," "most dear to men," one "whose long arms seize the liar," who "injures no one and is everyone's friend," one who was all-seeing and all-knowing — the sun was his "eye" on the world.

Mithra was responsible also for bringing rain, vegetation and health — for in the ancient eastern mind, it is the moral behavior of persons (especially the king) that determines the national welfare and brings a fertile climate. If the king in your land broke a treaty, you would be advised to pack up if you were a farmer, because Mithra would soon be gliding in on his chariot with a boar shape on the front (accompanied by a divine sidekick representing Victory) to kick some tail and put things right [MS.27-51].

At other times Mithra was paired with a deity named Varuna, who was his superior. Varuna was the god in charge of helping men cultivate rice (although rice "ripening in the untilled soil" was still Mithra's business), so the two of them together oversaw the agricultural aspects of men's lives.
The ancient Mithra was a great guy. Lord of the Contract, Upholder of Truth. Peaceful, benevolent, protector, provider of a nice place to live and cattle, not easily provoked. A little later in Aryan history, he did become more of a warrior (previously, he had left a lot of the tail-kicking duties to Varuna), but then switched back to pacifism.

But then Zoroastrianism came along, and Mithra had some

new things to do. He served as mediator between Ohrmazd and Ahriman, the good and bad gods of Zoroastrian dualism; but at the same time, he underwent something of a demotion as he became one of a group of seven lesser *yazatas* who served the upper-level deities [Cum.MM, 5] and was assigned some special escort duties: bringing demons to hell, and bringing souls to Paradise.

For a while after, things seem to have been quiet for Mithra. As late as the first century BC, Mithra is still associated with the sun along with Apollos and Hermes. [MS.129] So, why all this background? The problem was that Cumont was entirely wrong about very ancient (we shall say for convenience, Iranian) Mithraism being in continuity with Roman Mithraism.

For you see, the Roman Mithra was best known for his act of slaying a bull; yet there is no indication that the Iranian Mithra ever made his way into a bullpen for any reason. [MS, xiii] The Roman Mithra didn't appear at all interested in contract enforcement or escorting demons into hell. (Most likely, because demons are terrible tippers.) And to make matters more complex, his followers in Iran, unlike the Roman Mithraists, did not worship in cave-like rooms (although Porphyry did think, incorrectly, that Zoroaster, the "putative founder of the cult," originated the idea of a cave as the image of the cosmos — Beck.PO, 8), design levels of initiation, or pursue secrecy. [Ulan.OMM, 8]

There was simply no solid connection between the two faiths except for the name of the central god, some terminology, and astrological lore of the sort that was widely imported into the Roman Empire from Babylon anyway [Beck.PO, 87].

Nevertheless, because Cumont was locked into the notion of continuity, he assumed (for example) that the Iranian Mithra must have done some bull-slaying somewhere along the line, and he molded the evidence to fit his thesis, straining to find an Iranian myth *somewhere* that involved a bull-killing (it was done not by Mithra, but by Ahriman) and supposing that there was some connection or unknown story where the Iranian Mithra killed a bull.

Cumont's student Vermaseren [Ver.MSG, 17-18] also tried to find a connection, but the closest he could get was a story in which Soma, the god of life (who, as *rain*, was described as the *semen* of the sacred bull fertilizing the earth), was murdered by a consortium of gods which *included* Mithra — as a very reluctant participant who had to be convinced to go along with the plan.

But simply put, the Roman Mithra wasn't anything like the Iranian one. He dressed really sporty, with a Phrygian cap (typical headgear for Orientals of the day) and a flowing cape that would have made Superman green with envy. He slayed a cosmic bull and earned the worship and respect of the sun god. He had new friends, animals that gave him a helping hand (or paw, or claw) with the bull-slaying, as well as two torch-bearing twins who could have passed for his sons.

If this was the Iranian Mithra, he obviously went through a midlife crisis at some point. The only thing that remained the same was that Mithra kept a loose association with the sun, which was something many gods had.

By the time of the First International Congress of Mithraic Studies in the early 70s, the lack of evidence of an Iranian/Roman continuity led Mithraic scholars to suspect that Roman Mithraism was "a new creation using old

Iranian names and details for an exotic coloring to give a
suitably esoteric appearance to a mystery cult" [MS, xiii]
— and that Roman Mithraism was Mithraism in name only,
merely a new system that used the name of a known
ancient Eastern deity to attract urbane Romans who found
the east and all of its accoutrements an enticing mystery.
Think of it as repackaging an old religion to suit new tastes,
only all you keep is the name of the deity!

And what was that new religion? For years Mithraic
scholars puzzled over the meaning of the bull-slaying
scene; the problem was, as we have noted, that the
Mithraists left behind pictures without captions. Thus in the
70s, one scholar of Mithraism lamented [MS.437]:

> At present our knowledge of both general
> and local cult practice in respect of rites of
> passage, ceremonial feats and even
> underlying ideology is based more on
> conjecture than fact.

And Cumont himself observed, in the 50s [Cum.MM, 150,
152]:

> The sacred books which contain the prayers
> recited or chanted during the [Mithraic]
> survives, the ritual on the initiates, and the
> ceremonials of the feasts, have vanished and
> left scarce a trace behind...[we] know the
> esoteric disciplines of the Mysteries only
> from a few indiscretions.

But before too long, Mithraic scholars noticed something
(or actually, revived something first posited in 1869 that
Cumont, because of his biases, dismissed — Ulan.OMM,
15) about the bull-slaying scene: The various human,
animal, and other figures comprised a *star-map*! The bull
corresponded with Taurus; the scorpion coincided with

Scorpio; the dog matched up with Canis Major, and so on.

What Mithra himself corresponded to took a bit longer to decide; Spiedel first made a case for a correspondence with Orion [Spie.MO], but Ulansey has led the way with the thesis that Mithra is here to be identified with Perseus [Ulan.OMM, 26ff], and that Roman Mithraism was founded upon a "revolutionary" discovery in ancient astronomy (which was closely linked to astrology in that time) that "the entire cosmic structure was moving in a way which no one had even known before" — a process we now call the precession of the equinoxes.

In line with the Stoic belief that a divine being was the "source of every natural force," the personifying of natural forces in the form of mythical divine figures, and the origin on the cult in Tarsus, a city long under Persian domination and where Perseus was the leading god, Perseus was the perfect choice — but this wasn't the type of thing that the cultists wanted *everyone* to know about, so, Ulansey theorizes, they chose the name of Mithra (a Persian god), partly to cover the identity of Perseus (who was often associated with Persia), partly because of an alliance between the Ciclian pirates who first introduced Mithraism to the Romans and a leader in Asia Minor named Mithridates ("given of Mithra"). [Ulan.OMM, 89]

What has been the point of this diversion? The point is to give the reader a warning, to be on the lookout any time a critic makes some claim about Mithraism somehow being a parallel to Christianity. Check their sources carefully. If they cite source material from the Cumont or pre-Cumont era, then chances are excellent that *they are using material that is either greatly outdated, or else does not rely on sound scholarship* (i.e., prior to Cumont; works by the likes of King, Lajard, and Robertson).

Furthermore, if they have asserted anything at all definitive about Mithraic belief, they are probably wrong about it, and certainly basing it on the conjectures of someone who is either not a Mithraic specialist or else is badly outdated.

Mithraic scholars, you see, do not hold a candle for the thesis that Christianity borrowed anything philosophically from Mithraism, and they do not see any evidence of such borrowing, with one major exception: "The only domain in which we can ascertain in detail the extent to which Christianity imitated Mithraism is that of art." [MS.508n]

We are talking here not of apostolic Christianity, note well, but of Christianity in the third and fourth centuries, which, in an effort to prove that their faith was the superior one, embarked on an advertising campaign reminiscent of our soft drink wars. Mithra was depicted slaying the bull while riding its back; the church did a lookalike scene with Samson killing a lion. Mithra sent arrows into a rock to bring forth water; the church changed that into Moses getting water from the rock at Horeb. (Hmm, did the Jews copy that one?)

Think of how popular Pokemon is, and then think of the church as the one doing the Digimon ripoff — although one can't really bellow about borrowing in this case, for this happened in an age when art usually was imitative — it was a sort of one-upsmanship designed as a competition, and the church was not the only one doing it. Furthermore, it didn't involve an exchange or theft of ideology.

As to any other parallels, in the late 60s, before the coming of age of the astrological thesis, appeal was made to the "possibility of Mithraic influence" as appearing "in many instances" — and then again, the idea that Mithraism borrowed from Christianity was said to have "not been taken seriously enough into consideration." [Lae.MO, 86]

But regarded as more likely in any case was that the two systems "could have spoken to a Roman condition, a social need, and a theological question without having known of each other's existence."

As in so many other instances of philosophy and literature, parallel thoughts and social patterns can appear independently of one another as 'new' elements with the authentic consciousness of such newness."[ibid.] But such parallels have not been so much as suggested in the wake of the astrological thesis. Today (and even by Cumont) the parallels drawn between the two faiths (by *professional Mithraic scholars*) are almost entirely either "universal" religious traits (i.e., both had a moral code; what religion doesn't!?) or sociological: Both spread rapidly because of the "political unity and moral anarchy of the Empire." [Cum.MM, 188-9] Both drew large numbers from the lower classes. (And of course, numerous differences are cited as well: Christianity was favored in urban areas habited by the Jewish diaspora, whereas Mithraism was indifferent to Judaism and was popular in rural areas; Mithraism appealed to slaves, troops, and functionaries vs. Christianity's broader appeal; etc.)

It's a Conspiracy?
You may ask whether the copycat theorists know of any of this newer work on Mithraism by Mithraic scholars, and if so what they make of it. The answer is yes, they are becoming aware of it; but what they make of it is no more than a conspiracy. In her latest effort Acharaya says of the star-map thesis, and the lack of evidence that Mithra in his Iranian period ever slew a bull:

> The argument is in the main unconvincing
> and seems to be motivated by Christian
> backlash attempting to debunk the well-

founded contention that Christianity copied
Mithraism in many germane details.

At the point when scholars like Ulansey are implicitly
accused, as here, of being "motivated by Christian
backlash" (or as elsewhere, of being covert Christians!), the
critics are clearly holding a counsel of despair.

We are told, "In reality, the bull-slaying motif and ritual
existed in numerous cultures prior to the Christian era,
regardless of whether or not it is depicted in literature or
iconography in Persia." No one doubts that the bull-slaying
motif existed; the question is whether it appears as
something that Mithra did in the pre-Roman era, and the
other instances are completely meaningless in this context.
Ulansey shows that Mithra's act was related to the
discovery of the precession of the equinoxes; Acharya
offers the response that:

> In fact, the bull motif is a reflection of the
> Age of Taurus, around 4500-2300 BCE, one
> of the 2,150-year ages created by the
> precession of the equinoxes. The
> presumption by scholars is that the
> precession of the equinoxes was only
> "discovered" during the second century
> BCE by the Greek scientist Hipparchus;
> nevertheless, it is quite evident that the
> precession was well known, by the ruling
> elite and priestly faction, for millennia prior
> to its purported "discovery." That the
> ancients followed precessional ages is
> revealed abundantly in the archaeological
> record.

In stating this, Acharya places herself against not only
Ulansey, but as Ulansey states, historians of science who

agree that Hipparchus was the discoverer of the precession [Ulan.OMM, 76] — as well as against evidence from Aristotle and others showing that such knowledge was not known prior to Hipparchus [ibid., 79]. She posits otherwise unknown and unnamed "ruling elite" and "priests" who allegedly knew about the precession; yet when it comes to details, all she has to offer is one example: "The change between the ages of Taurus and Aries is recorded even in the Bible, at Exodus 12, where Moses institutes the sacrifice of the lamb or ram instead of the bull."

The problem here at face value is that even if true, this would be in the wrong order, if Ulansey is correct: If Exodus is symbolizing the precession, it should be ordering the sacrifice of the bull instead of the ram, not vice versa, for the bull was killed according to Ulansey's record c. 300 BC. Not that it matters, since Exodus 12, the implementation of Passover, says nothing about bulls, as "instead ofs" or for any other reason, and a lamb is still not a ram by any stretch of the imagination. Achraya is blowing bubbles here.

That "Dupuis insisted upon the identification, as did Volney," is a nice personal insight into their lives, but means nothing. Bunsen's wild speculations also are without grounding; to wit: "Like Ormuzd, Mithras is represented riding on the bull, and Jehovah is described as riding on the Cherub, Kirub or bull." Mithras is nowhere shown riding a bull; he is on the bull's back, killing it; on the other end, where is it, and when, that Jehovah is said to be riding a cherub, and how, linguistically, does this get to "bull"? Solar myths in which other gods of no relation to Mithra (Apis, etc.) are depicted as or called bulls, and sacrifices of bulls in various places, are of no relevance to the issue; merely asserting that they are "essentially the same motif as Mithra slaying the bull" and quoting another of like mind does not make it so — especially since there is no iconographic or literary evidence to prove this point.

Priming the Pump with Parallels?

We are now ready to embark upon the practical part of our essay in which we consider in turn each of the claims made of alleged "parallels" between Mithraism and Christianity.

Mithra was born of a virgin on December 25th in a cave, and his birth was attended by shepherds.

This claim is a mix of truth and obfuscations. Let's begin with the December 25th part by noting Glenn Miller's reply, which is more than sufficient: "...the Dec 25 issue is of no relevance to us--nowhere does the NT associate this date with Jesus' birth at all." This is something the later church did, wherever they got the idea from — not the apostolic church, and if there was any borrowing at all, everyone did it, for Dec. 25th was "universally distinguished by sacred festivities" [Cum.MM, 196] being that it was (at the time) the winter solstice.

Next, the cave part. First of all, Mithra was *not* born of a virgin in a cave; he was born *out of solid rock*, which presumably left a cave behind — and I suppose technically the rock he was born out of could have been classified as a virgin!

Here is how one Mithraic scholar describes the scene on Mithraic depictions: Mithra "wearing his Phrygian cap, issues forth from the rocky mass. As yet only his bare torso is visible. In each hand he raises aloft a lighted torch and, as an unusual detail, red flames shoot out all around him from the *petra genetrix*." [MS.173] Mithra was born a grown-up, but you won't hear the copycatters mention this! The rock-birth scene itself was a likely carryover from Perseus, who experienced a similar birth in an underground cavern. (Ulan.OMM, 36)

I'll add here that it is no help to appeal to similar abuses of the term "virgin" by church writers who tried to force an illicit parallel between Jesus and Adam. All they're doing is abusing and misusing the term the same way that "copycat" theorists are. So likewise, later instances of syncretism are of no value for the case (e.g., the infant Jesus depicted within an egg shape, which reflects the church's assumption of symbols as the "winner" in an ideological struggle — see below on art).

That leaves the shepherds, and this is one that is entirely true; although the shepherds did more than "attend" (unlike Luke's shepherds, they were witnesses to the birth; there was no angelic mediator), they also helped Mithra out of the rock, and offered him the first-fruits of their flock — quite a feat for these guys in any event, considering that Mithra's birth took place at a time when (oops!) men had supposedly not been created on earth yet. [Cum.MM, 132]

But the clincher here is that this scene, like nearly *all* Roman Mithraic evidence, dates at least *a century after* the time of the New Testament. It is too late to say that any "borrowing" was done by the Christian church — if there was any, it was the other way around; but there probably was none.

Mother Matters

The Iranian Mithra didn't have a "born out of rock" story; his conception was attributed, variously, to an incestuous relationship between Ahura-Mazda and his mother, or to the plain doings of an ordinary mortal woman...but there is no virgin conception/birth story to speak of. [Cum.MM, 16]

Acharya says that the Indian Mithra, "was born of a female, Aditi, the 'mother of the gods,' the inviolable or virgin dawn; this is simply yet another case of her applying terminology [a "dawn" as "virgin" — so when does the dawn start "having sex" and how?] illicitly. So likewise this word game: "It could be suggested that Mithra was born of 'Prima Materia,' or 'Primordial Matter,' which could also be considered 'First Mother,' 'Virgin Matter,' 'Virgin Mother,' etc..." — it can be "considered" no such thing except by vivid imagination; merely playing on the psycho-linguistic similarity of sound in the English words "matter" and "mother" and trying to equate "first" with "virgin" isn't going to do the job.

Research Assistant Punkish adds: ADITI (according to an astrological website) means Free unbound. Boundless heaven as compared with the finite earth. A Vedic goddess representing the primeval generator of all that emanated. The eternal space of boundless whole, the unfathomable depth signifying the veil over the unknown. (Note, not matter/mother but generator of matter!) The Rig Veda describes it as the father and mother of all gods; it is named Devamatri, mother of all gods, or Swabhavat, that which exists by itself. She is frequently implored for blessing children and cattle, for protection and forgiveness.

In the Yajur Veda, Aditi is addressed as the support of the sky, the sustainer of the earth, the sovereign of this world, and the wife of Vishnu. The Vishnu Purana describes Aditi, the daughter of Daksha and the wife of Kashyapa, to be the mother of 8 Adityas (q.v.). Wife of Vishnu or Kashyapa? A bit unlikely to be virginal then! Then we have this website Dialogueonline.net - Magazine (comparative research on major religions) where we find: "According to the Rigveda (10/72/2) Brahmanaspati, like a craftsman, created the gods, and the gods in turn created 'Sat' from 'Asat'.

The Rigveda (10/72/4-5) further says, "Daksha was born of

Aditi and Aditi was born of Daksha, the gods were born of Aditi and Aditi gave birth to eight sons". This mantra suggests mainly two things - first, Aditi and Daksha took birth of each other, which proposition is never possible; second, the Creator of this universe was Aditi because she gave birth to the gods. But it ridicules more brazenly when refuting such points Rigveda (8/90/15) says: "Aditi was daughter of Adityas".

In this connection, Rigveda produces more than one controversy as Rigveda tots up that Aditi was mother of Vishnu and so Rigveda (4/55/3 8/27/5) clarifies, "Aditi mothered Vishnu". But repudiating the same verse Vajasaney Samhita (20/60) and Taitirya Samhita (7/5/14) consolidates that Aditi was wife of Vishnu. The goddess, who herself is found in various controversies, is considered creator of this universe. Thus, these mantras fail to shed any meaningful light on the basic issue of the birth, motherhood and even creation of the universe by Aditi. (Creator And Creation In Hindu Perspective)

Acharya now adds in her work iconographic evidence allegedly showing "the babe Mithra seated in the lap of his virgin mother, with the gift-bearing Magi genuflecting in front of them." One is constrained to ask how an icon reflects that Mithra's mother was a virgin, since it is obviously not stated. One also wants to know if any of this evidence is pre-Christian (it is not). Quoting others who merely say it is indicating a virgin birth, yet offer no more evidence, is not an argument.
Finally, we are told of the "largest near-eastern Mithraeum [which] was built in western Persia at Kangavar, dedicated to 'Anahita, the Immaculate Virgin Mother of the Lord Mithras'." This is a very curious claim which is repeated around the Internet, but no source is given for it, and Acharya attributes it to a "writer" with no name or source.

I believe, however, that I have found the terminal source, and it is a paper written in 1993 by a then-high school student, David Fingrut, who made this claim without any documentation whatsoever himself. His paper is now posted on the Net as a text file.

That said, it is inaccurate to start with, since the building at Kanagvar is not a Mithraeum at all, but a temple to Anahita (dated 200 BC), and although I have found one source of untested value that affirms that Anahita was depicted as a virgin (in spite of being a fertility goddess!), she is regarded not at Mithra's mother, but as his consort (though it does offer other contradictory info) — and it knows nothing of such an inscription as described; and the mere existence of the goddess Anahita before the Roman era proves nothing.[73]

Another fraudulent attempt to validate this claim has been made by connecting it to a "Professor, M. Moghdam" who allegedly wrote a paper that was supposedly part of the Second International Congress of Mithraic Studies. It wasn't, as a check of the contents showed. This professor is also alleged to have edited a book entitled Iran: Elements of Destiny, which does relate this claim, but as far as can be determined, this is an entirely different person and not a genuine Mithraic scholar. The book itself is written by a photographer and makes the claim with no documentation or illustration. Finally, other sources that make this claim add such qualifications as, "Anahita was said to have conceived the Saviour [Mithra] from the seed of Zarathustra preserved in the waters of Lake Hamun in the Persian province of Sistan." Virginal conception? Please.

Table for Twelve?
Acharya in her latest now acknowledges that Mithra's

dozen are the zodiac, but goes on the defense by saying,
"the motif of the 12 disciples or followers in a 'last supper'
is recurrent in the Pagan world, including within
Mithraism" — with the Mithraic supper compared to the
Last Supper (see below). She also adds: "The Spartan King
Kleomenes had held a similar last supper with twelve
followers four hundred years before Jesus." This last
assertion is made by Plutarch in Parallel Lives, 'Agis and
Kleomenes' 37:2-3."

This is only partly true — I was alerted to this passage by a
helpful reader: "For [Cleomenes] sacrificed, and gave them
large portions, and, with a garland upon his head, feasted
and made merry with his friends. It is said that he began the
action sooner than he designed, having understood that a
servant who was privy to the plot had gone out to visit a
mistress that he loved. This made him afraid of a discovery;
and therefore, as soon as it was full moon, and all the
keepers sleeping off their wine, he put on his coat, and
opening his seam to bare his right shoulder, with his drawn
sword in his hand, he issued forth, together with his friends
provided in the same manner, making thirteen in all."
It's a "last supper," but it isn't invested with any
significance in itself (least of all, atoning significance! —
and these guys clearly had to have a "last meal" at some
point!), and the twelve companions don't have any real role
beyond this pericope. We'd put this one down as natural
coincidence (as there are people with five, 10, or other
numbers of companions as well).

Is That the Best Authority?
Tekton Research Associate Punkish has added this: ...[T]he
footnote [in Christ Conspiracy] reads O'Hara, which in the
bibliography is Gwydion O'Hara, Sun Lore. Now if you
look this guy up on Amazon.com you find his book reviews
are not very positive, in fact he's the sort of person, like

Barbara Walker, who makes things up. What kind of authority is he? He isn't: he's a writer on pagan practices and he was once a high priest of the Wiccan Church of Canada at a time when it was an ideal rather than a reality (!)...sounds like another nut. What's Acharya doing using this guy instead of a Mithraic scholar?

Additional Points From Freke and Gandy

Research Assistant Punkish adds these points concerning what is said about Mithra in The Jesus Mysteries: Having accomplished his mission on Earth, Mithras was said to have ascended to heaven in a sun-chariot - and the footnote refers you to Cumont, p138. Cumont is actually referring to Mithra watching over the first couple (a sort of Adam and Eve) and providing divine protection to humanity during a Noahlike flood! Not related to Jesus' mission, though omission of these details implies such, especially during a resurrection discussion.

As for Mithras ascending to heaven, this is a misreading of the text. It is not Mithra, but the gods (e.g. Helios) with him who after looking after the humans, ascend, then Mithras crosses the Ocean in his chariot. The Ocean tries to engulf him and fails, and finally he joins the immortals' habitation. The term "ascension" is not uniquely applied to Mithras by Cumont.

JM's claims to Christian eschatology parallels: they list, Mithras as right hand authority, God of Light, ruler of the world, waiting for End of Time, return to earth, awake dead & pass judgment. Footnote 258 p271 says "Cumont collates a mass of Mithraic eschatological doctrines identical to Christianity." This is a terrible misreading of Cumont pp145-146...I can't find anything about "ruler of the world", protector of humanity yes, ruler no.

While Mithras is said to redescend together with a bull and separates the good from the bad (as "god of truth", not God of Light - the nearest we get is his title as the celestial father who receives the faithful in a resplendent mansion!), he sacrifices the bull before the assembled humanity which are raised from the dead yes, but the doctrine is an add-on to the immortal soul view - which sounds more like transmigration, and the resurrection is for the purpose of material enjoyment.

The bull's fat and consecrated wine [not its blood] is offered to the just to gain immortality - yet it is Ormazd who executes the judgment - as annihilation of the wicked together with the destruction, not eternal punishment, of Ahriman and his demons, and a rejuvenated universe is the future happiness without evil. How is this identical to Christian eschatology as Freke and Gandy have claimed?

He was considered a great traveling teacher and master.

Aside from the fact that this is what we would expect from *any* major leadership figure, especially in a religious context ("He was a great god — he taught us *nothing!*"), I have to say that this looks to be the first of several outright "ringers" in the set. I have found *nowhere* any indication that Mithra was a teacher, traveling or otherwise. (He probably could be called a "master," but what leading figure would not be? And a master in what sense? This is rather a vague parallel to draw!)

At any rate, since there is no evidence for this one in any of the Mithraic literature, we issue our first challenge to the pagan-copycat theorists: How is it shown that Mithra was a "great traveling teacher"? What did he teach, and where, and to whom? How was he a "master" and why is this a similarity to Jesus?

He had 12 companions or disciples.

I have seen this claim repeated a number of times, almost always (see below) without any documentation. (One of our readers wrote to Acharya asking for specific evidence of this one...she did not reply, although she had readily replied to a prior message.) The Iranian Mithras, as we have seen, did have a single companion (Varuna), and the Roman Mithra had two helper/companions, tiny torch-bearing likenesses of himself, called Cautes and Cautopatres, that were perhaps meant to represent the sunrise and sunset (whereas "Big Daddy" Mithra was supposed to be noon), spring and autumn, the stars Albedaran and Antares [Beck.PO, 26] or life and death.

(Freke and Gandy attempt to link these twins to the two thieves crucified with Jesus! - Frek.JM, 51 - because one went to heaven with Jesus [torch up] and one went to hell [torch down]!) Mithra also had a number of animal companions: a snake, a dog, a lion, a scorpion — but not 12 of them.
Now here's an irony. My one idea as to where they got this one was a picture of the bull-slaying scene carved in stone, found in Ulansey's book, that depicts the scene framed by 2 vertical rows with 6 pictures of what seem to be human figures or faces on each side. It occurred to me that some non-Mithraist perhaps saw this picture and said, "Ah ha, those 12 people must be companions or disciples! Just like Jesus!"

Days later I received Freke and Gandy's book, and sure enough — that's how they make the connection. Indeed, they go as far as saying that during the Mirthaic initiation ceremony, Mithraic disciples dressed up as the signs of the zodiac and formed a circle around the initiate. [Frek.JM, 42] Where they (or rather, their source) get this information about the methods of Mithraic initiation, one can only guess: No Mithraic scholar seems aware of it, and their source, Godwin, is a specialist in "Western esoteric teaching" — not a Mithraist, and it shows, because although writing in 1981, well after the first Mithraic congress, Godwin was still following Cumont's line that Iranian and Roman Mithraism were the same, and thus ended up offering interpretations of the bull-slaying scene that bear no resemblance to what Mithraic scholars today see in it at all.

To be fair, though, Freke and Gandy do not give the page number where Godwin supposedly says this — and his material on Mithraism says nothing about any initiation ceremony. However, aside from the fact that this carving is (yet again!) significantly post-Christian (so that any borrowing would have had to be the other way around), these figures have been identified by modern Mithraic scholars as representing zodiacal symbols. Indeed, the top two faces are supposed to be the sun and the moon! (See also a similar carving herein)

Mithra's followers were promised immortality.

This one is no more than a guess, although probably a good one: As one Mithraic scholar put it, Mithraism "surely offered its initiates deliverance from some awful fate to which all other men were doomed, and a privileged passage to some ultimate state of well-being." [MS.470]
Why is this a good guess? Not because Mithraism borrowed from Christianity, or Christianity borrowed from Mithraism, or anyone borrowed from anyone, but because if you don't promise your adherents *something* that secures their eternity, you may as well give up running a religion and go and sell timeshares in Alaska!

In practical terms, however, the only hard evidence of a "salvational" ideology is a piece of graffiti found in the Santa Prisca Mithraeum (a Mithraist "church" building, if you will), dated no earlier than *200 AD*, that reads, "And us, too, you saved by spilling the eternal blood." [Spie.MO, 45; Gor.IV, 114n; Verm.MSG, 172] Note that this refers to Mithra spilling the blood of the *bull* — not his own — and that (according to the modern Mithraic "astrological" interpretation) this does *not* mean "salvation" in a Christian sense (involving freedom from sin) but an ascent through levels of initiation into immortality.

He performed miracles.

Mithra did perform a number of actions rather typical for any deity worldwide, true or false, and in both his Iranian and Roman incarnations. But this is another one of those things where we just say, "What's the big deal?" We agree with Miller:

> *It must be remembered that SOME general similarities MUST apply to any religious leader. They must generally be good leaders, do noteworthy feats of goodness and/or supernatural power, establish teachings and traditions, create community rituals, and overcome some forms of evil. These are common elements of the religious life—NOT objects that require some theory of dependence...The common aspect of homo religiosus is an adequate and more plausible explanation than dependence.*

Of course, our pagan-copycat theorists are welcome to try and draw more exact parallels, but as yet I have seen no cited example where Mithra turned water into wine or calmed a storm.

As the "great bull of the Sun," Mithra sacrificed himself for world peace.

This description is rather spun out into a sound-alike of Christian belief, but behind the vagueness lies a different story. Mithra did not "sacrifice himself" in the sense that he died; he was not the "great bull of the Sun", but rather, he killed the bull (attempts to somehow identify Mithra with the very bull he slayed, although popular with outdated non-Mithraists like Loisy and Bunsen, were rejected by Vermaseren, who said that "neither the temples nor the inscriptions give any definite evidence to support this view and only future finds can confirm it" [Verm.MSG, 103]; it was not for the sake of "world peace" (except, perhaps, in the sense that Cumont interpreted the bull-slaying as a creation myth [Cum.MM, 193], in which he was entirely wrong).

Mithra could only be said to have "sacrificed himself" in the sense that he went out and took a risk to do a heroic deed; the rest finds no justification at all in modern Mithraic studies literature — much less does it entail a parallel to Christ, who sacrificed himself for atonement from personal sin (not "world peace").

He was buried in a tomb and after three days rose again. His resurrection was celebrated every year.

I have to classify these two as "ringers" — I see no references anywhere in the Mithraic studies literature to Mithra being buried, or even dying, for that matter [Gordon says directly, that there is "no death of Mithras" — Gor.III, 96] and so of course no rising again and no "resurrection" (in a Jewish sense?!) to celebrate. Freke and Gandy [Frek.JM, 56] claim that the Mithraic initiates "enacted a similar resurrection scene", but their only reference is to a comment by Tertullian, significantly after New Testament times!

Tekton Research Assistant Punkish adds:
> *The footnote is for Tertullian's Prescription Against Heretics, chapter 40 which says, "if my memory still serves me, Mithra there (in the kingdom of Satan), sets his marks on the foreheads of his soldiers; celebrates also the oblation of bread, and introduces an image of a resurrection, and before a sword wreathes a crown"...so their argument relies on Tertullian's memory, and it isn't the initiates but Mithra who does the celebrating and introduces an *image* of a resurrection! How is that at all related to initiates acting out a scene?*

Wynne-Tyson [Wyn.MFC, 24; cf. Ver.MSG, 38] also refers to a church writer of the *fourth* century, Firmicus, who says that the Mithraists mourn the image of a dead Mithras — still way too late! — but after reading the work of Firmicus, I find no such reference at all.

He was called "the Good Shepherd" and identified with both the Lamb and the Lion.

Only the third aspect has any truth to it as far as I can find from Mithraic studies sources: The lion was regarded in Roman Mithraism as Mithra's "totem" animal, just as Athena's animal was the owl and Artemis' animal was the deer [Biv.PM, 32]. Since Mithra was a sun-god, there was also an association with Leo, which was the House of the Sun in Babylonian astrology.

But aside from this evidence all being post-Christian, one

may ask what the big deal is. Do we expect the Christians or the Mithraists to say, "Darn, we can't use the lion, it's already taken by the other guys?" Should Exxon give up their tiger because of Frosted Flakes? But if you really want to get technical, Jesus owned the rights to the lion symbol as a member of the tribe of Judah long before Mithras even appeared in his Iranian incarnation (Gen. 49:9).

There are other associations as well: In the Roman material, one of Mithra's companions in the bull-slaying scene is a lion; the lion is sometimes Mithra's hunting and feasting companion; Mithra is sometimes associated with a lion-*headed* being who is sometimes identified as the evil Zoroastrian god Ahriman [MS.277]; one of the seven stages of initiation in Mithraism is the lion stage.

Mithra is only *called* a lion in one Mithraic tale (which is part of *Armenian* folklore — where did the writers of the NT pick that up?) because as a child he killed a lion and split it in two. [MS.356, 442]

He was considered the "Way, the Truth and the Light," and the "Logos," "Redeemer," "Savior" and "Messiah." Acharya now adds in her latest work the titles creator of the world, God of gods, the mediator, mighty ruler, king of gods, lord of heaven and earth, Sun of Righteousness.

We have several titles here, and yes, though I searched through the works of Mithraic scholars, I found none of these applied to Mithra, other than the role of mediator (not, though, in the sense of a mediator between God and man because of sin, but as a mediator between Zoroaster's good and evil gods; we have seen the "sun" identification, but never that title) — not even the new ones were ever listed by the Mithraic scholars.

There is a reference to a "Logos" that was *taught* to the

Mithraic initiates [MS.206](in the Roman evidence, which is again, significantly after the establishment of Christianity), but let it be remembered that "logos" means "word" and goes back earlier in Judaism to Philo — Christians borrowed the idea from Philo, perhaps, or from the general background of the word, but not from Mithraism.

His sacred day was Sunday, the "Lord's Day," hundreds of years before the appearance of Christ.
Mithra had his principal festival of what was later to become Easter.

We'll consider these two together. The Iranian Mithra had a few special celebrations: a festival on October 8; another on September 12-16, and a "cattle-pairing" festival on October 12-16 [MS.59]. But as for an Easter festival, I have seen only that there was *a* festival at the spring equinox — and it was one of just four, one for each season.

In terms of Sunday being a sacred day, this is correct [Cum.MM, 190-1], but it only appears in Roman Mithraism, and the argument here is apparently assuming, like Cumont, that what held true for Roman Mithraism also held true for the Iranian version — but there is no evidence for this. If any borrowing occurred (it probably didn't), it was the other way around.

His religion had a eucharist or "Lord's Supper," at which Mithra said, "He who shall not eat of my body nor drink of my blood so that he may be one with me and I with him, shall not be saved."

It took me some digging to discover the actual origin of this saying. Godwin says that the reference is from a "Persian Mithraic text," but does not give the dating of this text, nor does he say where it was found, nor is any documentation offered. I finally found something in Vermaseren [Verm.MSG, 103] — the source of this saying is a *medieval* text; and the speaker is *not* Mithras, but Zarathustra!

Although Vermaseren suggested that this might be the formula that Justin referred to (but did not describe at all) as being part of the Mithraic "Eucharist," there is no evidence for the saying prior to this medieval text.

Critics try to give the rite some ancestry by claiming that it derives from an Iranian Mithraic ceremony using a psychadelic plant called Haoma, but they are clearly grasping at straws and adding speculations of meaning in order to make this rite seem similar to the Eucharist. This piece of "evidence" is far, far too late to be useful — except as possible proof that Mithraism borrowed from Christianity! (Christianity of course was in Persia far earlier than this medieval text; see Martin Palmer's *Jesus Sutras* for details.[74])

The closest thing that Mithraism had to a "Last Supper" was the taking of staples (bread, water, wine and meat) by the Mithraic initiates, which was perhaps a celebration of the meal that Mithra had with the sun deity after slaying the bull. However, the meal of the initiates is usually seen as no more than a general fellowship meal of the sort that was practiced by groups all over the Roman world — from religious groups to funeral societies. [MS.348]

"His annual sacrifice is the passover of the Magi, a symbolical atonement or pledge of moral and physical regeneration."

This is rather a confused statement, for it compounds an

apparent falsity (I have found no indication that Mithra's "sacrifice" was annual, rather than a once-in-the-past event); it uses terms from Judeo-Christian belief ("passover", "atonement") to describe a rite from Mithraism, without showing any similarities at all. I see this as little more than a case of illicitly applying terminology, and until more detail is provided, it can be regarded as little else.

Shmuel Golding is quoted as saying that 1 Cor. 10:4 is "identical words to those found in the Mithraic scriptures, except that the name Mithra is used instead of Christ."

In response to this, I need to say that if Golding had some Mithraic scriptures in his possession, he needs to turn them over to Mithraic scholarly community at once, because they will want to know about them. Ulansey [Ulan.OMM, 3] tells us that "the teachings of the (Mithraic) cult were, as far as we know, never written down" and we "have been left with practically no literary evidence relating to the cult which would help (us) reconstruct its esoteric doctrines."

So where is Golding getting this from? (A reader also noted that Paul is alluding the the Old Testament book of Numbers; so how does that square with a Mithraic origin for this verse?)

The Catholic Encyclopedia is quoted as saying that Mithraic services were conduced by "fathers" and that the "chief of the fathers, a sort of pope, who always lived at Rome, was called 'Pater Patratus.'"

Other critics add their own idea: Like Christians, Mithraic initiates called each other "brother" [Frek.JM, 67]. Both claims are true, but quite simply, so what? The use of familial terms within religious societies is a universal, and that's no surprise, because familial terms are the most useful for expressing endearment or commitment. Indeed, "kinship terminology" was used in Greco-Roman antiquity for fellows of the same religion or race, as well as of friends, allies, and even prospective guests [Keener commentary on Matthew, 370n].

(I have seen no evidence that the Pater Patratus "always lived" at Rome, but even if he did, this would be of no moment: As the leading city of the Empire, where else would this person most likely have headquarters? This means no more than mainline churches all having headquarters in New York, or all foreign countries having embassies in Washington. Beyond that, we hardly need to defend "borrowing" when what is at stake is a church organizational structure that came into being many years after apostolic times.)

That ends our listing, and thus our conclusion: In not one instance has a convincing case been made that Christianity borrowed anything from Mithraism.

The evidence is either too late, not in line with the conclusions of modern Mithraic scholars, or just plain not there.

11/2012: We offer now some commentary from an informed reader who has been an archaeologist, and who in 1974 I assisted to an excavation of a Mithreum in former Yugoslavia.

I've followed developments ever since and I notice that apparently even the experts pay not enough attention to a much more significant dissimilarity with Christianity: Mithraism by all accounts was an on invitation only institution. You didn't ask to be admitted, you had to produce an invitation. To my knowledge there was no apostolate and no propaganda. Nevertheless the Mithraic societies spread rapidly and given their mode of operation perfectly legal. But the key feature here is that they were the one to choose you and not the other way around. Hence, despite of minuscule numbers, the Mithras people wielded a disproportionate influence and at one point pervaded the military ranks down to the subaltern charges.

Christianity on the other hand practiced an open door policy with only a token initiation procedure – which in itself must already have raised concerns with the authorities, if it didn't downright violate legislation, and it was actively disseminating propaganda.

In other words the Mithrea operated more like the lodges of modern Masons (no other comparison intended, just the modus operandi) than a religion for the masses. Although I do suspect that the Masonic loges and the Mithrea had and have something else in common: both don't really knew and know how and under what circumstances they originated and therefore made up traditions and mythologies as they went along. (The reader wishes to stress that the comparison with the Masons is merely a reference to a common modus operandi, not to similarities of myth or message. However considering how influential both organizations had been in their heydays one can also compare on whom they exercised their influence: the Mithrea recruited their members from the upper echelons of society and especially the military. Similar the Masons: the Metropolitan police in London has still about 5000 officers associated with the Masons, a member of the royal family is master of the grand lodge.)

There is also a legal point to consider: Christian gatherings without a licence from the authorities violated laws for the constitution of collegia – which could be anything: funeral

societies, banquet societies, cult societies, chambers of
commerce, or guilds. In all these instances a permit was
required by law and depending on the paranoia of a regime
at any given time disregard of the law could lead to
repercussions. Many details in the Paulines reflect on this
situation, when a formerly legal collegium (aka church)
was in danger to lose its status as a religio licta due to the
sudden influx of new members in large numbers. This
generated a great deal of bickering and heresy hunting
among the early Christians which then the later heresies
inherited and fully developed at a time when Christianity
was already religion of the state.

Mithraism managed to undercut the legal pitfalls. I give
you an example: the excavation site in Dura Europos shows
that it all started from a private house in pretty much
exactly 168 AD. (That's just Dura, I am not reaching here.)
There is an epigraph dedicated by Ethpeni, Commander of
the Palmyrian archers. In 170 AD another epigraph by a
certain Zenobius celebrates a modest renovation of the
shrine; in 210 AD there is an overhaul and enlargement by
Antonius Valentinus (now Dura II) and in 240 AD (Dura
III) an extensive alteration and enlargement, the painter of
the murals left his signature.
Now: what is striking here is the lack of architectural
uniformity among the various excavation sites – there
seems to be no requirement for consecrated ground or
particular alinements – elsewhere and in comparison with
Dura, while by the same token the iconography is not only
uniform but in all appearance derived from Italian models.
The largest Mithreum in Bad Altenburg in Austria – the
place where Diocletian demoted Constantine – was of
course commissioned by the state, but most of them seem
to have grown from private enterprises mostly by army
personnel and started at a very small scale – a good way of
circumventing Roman association laws and the military

rule book.

So, unlike the Masons, exclusivity was not so much a lure as a means to stay legal without the hassles of the licensing process.

Sources

Beck.PO — Beck, Roger. *Planetary Gods and Planetary Orders in the Mysteries of Mithras.* London: Brill, 1988.

Biv.PM — Bivar, A. D. *The Personalities of Mithra in Archaeology and Literature.* New York: Bibliotheca Persica Press, 1998.

Cum.MM — Cumont, Franz. *The Mysteries of Mithra.* New York: Dover, 1950.

Frek.JM — Freke, Timothy and Peter Gandy. *The Jesus Mysteries: Was the "Original Jesus" a Pagan God?* New York: Harmony Books, 1999.

Gor.IV — Gordon, Richard. *Image and Value in the Greco-Roman World.* Aldershot: Variorum, 1996.

Lae.MO — Laeuchli, Samuel. *Mithraism in Ostia: Mystery Religions and Christianity in the Ancient Port of Rome.* Northwestern U. Press, 1967.

MS — *Mithraic Studies: Proceedings of the First International Congress of Mithraic Studies.* Manchester U. Press, 1975.

Spei.MO — Spiedel, Michael. *Mithras-Orion, Greek Hero and Roman Army God.* Leiden: E. J. Brill, 1980.

Ulan.OMM — Ulansey, David. *The Origins of the Mithraic Mysteries: Cosmology and Salvation in the Ancient World.* New York: Oxford U. Press, 1989.<

Ver.MSG — Vermaseren, M. J. *Mithras the Secret God.* New York: Barnes and Noble, 1963.

Wyn.MFC — Wynne-Tyson, Esme. *Mithras: The Fellow in the Cap.* New York: Barnes and Noble, 1958.

Reader also recommends Iranica Online:
http://www.iranicaonline.org/articles/mithraism

Index

Atheism, 13

Atheist, 3, 13, 26, 27, 34,
41, 42, 45, 48, 52, 53,
55, 56, 63, 64, 67, 71,
75, 76, 79, 82, 87, 90,
100, 101, 102, 103,
111, 113, 115, 119,
120, 132, 134, 136,
139, 143, 147, 153, 164

Atheists, 4, 19, 26, 41,
71, 74, 75, 82, 101,
109, 119

Father, 7, 9, 10, 13, 19,
23, 24, 29, 31, 32, 41,
44, 49, 50, 56, 57, 61,
62, 63, 64, 65, 68, 69,
71, 76, 77, 78, 79, 80,
83, 95, 99, 103, 104,
109, 110, 113, 126,
130, 133, 134, 140,
141, 142, 143, 144,
146, 147, 148, 156,
157, 158, 159, 164, 165

God, 1

Guzikowski, 1, 3, 4, 5, 6,
9, 10, 11, 14, 15, 26,
32, 119, 159, 162, 163,
164, 166, 226

Mithra, 4, 26, 42, 43, 74,
117, 126, 127

Mithraic, 4, 5, 13, 25, 29,
31, 32, 41, 43, 57, 60,
66, 76, 81, 85, 87, 90,
118, 119, 120, 131,
136, 148

Mithraism, 4, 5, 19, 47,
51, 52, 79, 107, 111,
173, 191, 193, 195,
196, 197, 198, 199,
200, 201, 203, 208,
212, 215, 216, 217,
218, 219, 220, 222, 223

Mithras, 5, 42, 43, 52,
108, 116, 118

Mother, 7, 8, 9, 10, 11,
13, 19, 23, 24, 25, 26,
27, 29, 30, 32, 33, 34,
37, 41, 43, 44, 45, 47,
48, 49, 50, 51, 54, 56,
59, 61, 62, 63, 64, 65,
66, 67, 68, 69, 71, 74,
75, 76, 78, 79, 80, 81,
83, 85, 86, 87, 88, 89,
90, 92, 93, 95, 96, 99,
101, 103, 107, 113,
114, 115, 118, 119,
120, 121, 122, 123,
125, 126, 128, 130,
131, 132, 133, 134,
135, 140, 141, 143,
144, 146, 147, 148,
149, 152, 156, 157,
158, 159, 163, 164,
165, 166, 167

Occult, 8, 37, 42, 43, 54,
165, 166

Scott, 1, 3, 6, 7, 10, 149,
     156, 163, 226
Sol, 29, 42, 44, 47, 50,
     54, 56, 60, 61, 62, 66,
     67, 68, 71, 72, 73, 76,
     83, 103, 104, 106, 107,
     108, 109, 111, 113,
114, 115, 116, 118,
120, 121, 125, 126,
127, 129, 130, 131,
133, 134, 135, 136,
139, 140, 141, 144,
146, 147, 148, 149, 161

Endnotes

[1] Scott Myers, "Interview (Part 3): Aaron Guzikowski ('Prisoners')," *Go Into the Story*, April 22, 2015: https://gointothestory.blcklst.com/interview-part-3-aaron-guzikowski-prisoners-5b53e76f4cfd

[2] Simon Thompson, "Ridley Scott Talks 'Raised By Wolves' And The Future Of The 'Alien' Franchise," *Forbes*, September 2, 2020: https://www.forbes.com/sites/simonthompson/2020/09/02/ridley-scott-interview-raised-by-wolves-hbo-max-alien-franchise-future-sequel-news/#cf65e3058316

[3] Joe Deckelmeier, "Aaron Guzikowski Interview: Raised by Wolves," *ScreenRant*, September 15, 2020: https://screenrant.com/raised-wolves-aaron-guzikowski-interview

[4] See the Chris White research which debunks *Zeitgeist* in vast detail: https://conspiracyclothes.com/nowheretorun/?s=zeitgeist

[5] Meghan O'Keefe, "'Raised By Wolves' Creator Promises Big Answers by Season 1's Finale," *Decider*, September 3, 2020: https://decider.com/2020/09/03/raised-by-wolves-creator-lore-five-seasons-planned

[6] "Mithras past-present-future," *Carnaval*: http://www.carnaval.com/mithras

[7] Siddhant Adlakha, "Raised By Wolves Premiere: Breaking Down Ridley Scott's Latest Android Saga (SPOILERS)," *IGN*, September 4, 2020: https://www.ign.com/articles/raised-by-wolves-episode-1-2-3-mother-necromancer-mithraic-religion-sol

[8] Jennifer Vineyard, "'Raised by Wolves': Ridley Scott Explains That Monstrous Finale," *New York Times*, October 1, 2020: https://www.nytimes.com/2020/10/01/arts/television/raised-by-wolves-finale-ridley-scott.html

[9] Jennifer Vineyard, "'Raised by Wolves': Ridley Scott Explains That Monstrous Finale," *New York Times*, October 1, 2020: https://www.nytimes.com/2020/10/01/arts/television/raised-by-wolves-finale-ridley-scott.html

[10] Jacob Oller, "Raised by Wolves' creator wants to know what will 'lead us out of the darkness'," *SyFy*, September 3, 2020: https://www.syfy.com/syfywire/raised-by-wolves-hbo-max-aaron-guzikowski-ridley-scott

[11] Jennifer Vineyard, "'Raised by Wolves': Ridley Scott Explains That Monstrous Finale," *New York Times*, October 1, 2020: https://www.nytimes.com/2020/10/01/arts/television/raised-by-wolves-finale-ridley-scott.html

[12] Simon Thompson, "Ridley Scott Talks 'Raised By Wolves' And The Future Of The 'Alien' Franchise," *Forbes*, September 2, 2020: https://www.forbes.com/sites/simonthompson/2020/09/02/ridley-scott-interview-raised-by-wolves-hbo-max-alien-franchise-future-sequel-news/#cf65e3058316

[13] Jennifer Vineyard, "'Raised by Wolves': Ridley Scott Explains That Monstrous Finale," *New York Times*, October 1, 2020: https://www.nytimes.com/2020/10/01/arts/television/raised-by-wolves-finale-ridley-scott.html

[14] Ken Ammi's *TrueFreeThinker*'s articles featuring David Bowie: http://www.truefreethinker.com/search/luceneapi_node/%22David%20Bowie%22

[15] Jennifer Vineyard, "'Raised by Wolves': Ridley Scott Explains That Monstrous Finale," *New York Times*, October 1, 2020: https://www.nytimes.com/2020/10/01/arts/television/raised-by-wolves-finale-ridley-scott.html

[16] Gregory Ellwood, "'Raised By Wolves': Aaron Guzikowski On Atheists, Androids & World Building With Ridley Scott [Interview]," *The Playlist*, September 4, 2020: https://theplaylist.net/raised-by-wolves-aaron-guzikowski-interview-20200904

[17] Charles Trapunski, "Interview: Raised by Wolves' Amanda Collin," *Brieftake*, September 2, 2020: https://brieftake.com/interview-raised-by-wolves-amanda-collin

[18] Joe Deckelmeier, "Amanda Collin & Abubakar Salim Interview: Raised by Wolves," *ScreenRant*, September 16, 2020: https://screenrant.com/raised-wolves-amanda-collin-abubakar-salim-interview

[19] Charles Trapunski, "Interview: Raised by Wolves' Amanda Collin," *Brieftake*, September 2, 2020: https://brieftake.com/interview-raised-by-wolves-amanda-collin

[20] Joe Deckelmeier, "Amanda Collin & Abubakar Salim Interview: Raised by Wolves," *ScreenRant*, September 16, 2020: https://screenrant.com/raised-wolves-amanda-collin-abubakar-salim-interview

[21] AFP, "Ridley Scott brings Bowie and bodysuits to sci-fi TV debut 'Raised by Wolves,'" *MSN*, August 28, 2020: https://www.msn.com/en-us/movies/news/ridley-scott-brings-bowie-and-bodysuits-to-sci-fi-tv-debut-raised-by-wolves/ar-BB18u7i3

[22] Gregory Ellwood, "'Raised By Wolves': Aaron Guzikowski On Atheists, Androids & World Building With Ridley Scott [Interview]," *The Playlist*, September 4, 2020: https://theplaylist.net/raised-by-wolves-aaron-guzikowski-interview-20200904

[23] Joe Deckelmeier, "Aaron Guzikowski Interview: Raised by Wolves," *ScreenRant*, September 15, 2020: https://screenrant.com/raised-wolves-aaron-guzikowski-interview

[24] Joe Deckelmeier, "Travis Fimmel & Niamh Algar Interview: Raised by Wolves," *ScreenRant*, September 14, 2020: https://screenrant.com/raised-wolves-travis-fimmel-niamh-algor-interview

[25] Kristyn Clarke, "Raised By Wolves Interview: Travis Fimmel And Niamh Algar Share Details About Their Characters, Motivations And More!," *Age of the Nerd*, September 4, 2020: https://www.ageofthenerd.com/2020/09/raised-by-wolves-interview-travis-fimmel-and-niamh-algar-share-details-about-their-characters-motivations-and-more

[26] Joe Deckelmeier, "Travis Fimmel & Niamh Algar Interview: Raised by Wolves," *ScreenRant*, September 14, 2020: https://screenrant.com/raised-wolves-travis-fimmel-niamh-algor-interview

[27] Charles Trapunski, "Interview: Raised by Wolves' Amanda Collin," *Brieftake*, September 2, 2020: https://brieftake.com/interview-raised-by-wolves-amanda-collin

[28] Jacob Oller, "Raised by Wolves' creator wants to know what will 'lead us out of the darkness'," *SyFy*, September 3, 2020: https://www.syfy.com/syfywire/raised-by-wolves-hbo-max-aaron-guzikowski-ridley-scott

[29] Meghan O'Keefe, "'Raised By Wolves' Creator Promises Big Answers by Season 1's Finale," *Decider*, September 3, 2020: https://decider.com/2020/09/03/raised-by-wolves-creator-lore-five-seasons-planned

[30] Gregory Ellwood, "'Raised By Wolves': Aaron Guzikowski On Atheists, Androids & World Building With Ridley Scott [Interview]," *The Playlist*, September 4, 2020: https://theplaylist.net/raised-by-wolves-aaron-guzikowski-interview-20200904

[31] Samuel Spencer, "'Raised By Wolves' Ending Explained: Show Boss Breaks Down Season Finale," *Newsweek*, October 1, 2020: https://www.newsweek.com/raised-wolves-ending-explained-season-finale-aaron-guzikowski-interview-hbo-max-1535319

[32] Jennifer Vineyard, "'Raised by Wolves': Ridley Scott Explains That Monstrous Finale," *New York Times*, October 1, 2020: https://www.nytimes.com/2020/10/01/arts/television/raised-by-wolves-finale-ridley-scott.html

[33] Charles Trapunski, "Interview: Raised by Wolves' Amanda Collin," *Brieftake*, September 2, 2020: https://brieftake.com/interview-raised-

by-wolves-amanda-collin

34 Richard Dawkins, *River Out of Eden - A Darwinian View of Life* (New York, NY: Basic Books, 1995), p. 96

35 During his debate with Paul Manata

36 Jennifer Vineyard, "'Raised by Wolves': Ridley Scott Explains That Monstrous Finale," *New York Times*, October 1, 2020: https://www.nytimes.com/2020/10/01/arts/television/raised-by-wolves-finale-ridley-scott.html

37 Discordianism entry, *Wikipedia*: https://en.wikipedia.org/wiki/Discordianism, citing Robert Anton Wilson, *Cosmic Trigger I: Final Secret of the Illuminati* (Scottsdale, AZ: New Falcon Publications, 1992), p. 65

38 Samuel Spencer, "'Raised By Wolves' Ending Explained: Show Boss Breaks Down Season Finale," *Newsweek*, October 1, 2020: https://www.newsweek.com/raised-wolves-ending-explained-season-finale-aaron-guzikowski-interview-hbo-max-1535319

39 Gregory Ellwood, "'Raised By Wolves': Aaron Guzikowski On Atheists, Androids & World Building With Ridley Scott [Interview]," *The Playlist*, September 4, 2020: https://theplaylist.net/raised-by-wolves-aaron-guzikowski-interview-20200904

40 Dan Sarto, "MR. X Delivers Otherworldly VFX for Ridley Scott's 'Raised by Wolves,'" *Animation World Network*, October 21, 2020: https://www.awn.com/news/mr-x-delivers-otherworldly-vfx-ridley-scotts-raised-wolves

41 David Ulansey, "MITHRAISM: The Cosmic Mysteries of Mithras," *Mysterium*: http://www.mysterium.com/mithras.html

42 Ken Ammi, "Atheism and Rape - Walter Sinnott-Armstrong Elucidates," *TrueFreeThinker*: http://truefreethinker.com/articles/atheism-and-rape-walter-sinnott-armstrong-elucidates
Ken Ammi, "Sam Harris - The Rape Comments," *TrueFreeThinker*: http://truefreethinker.com/articles/sam-harris-rape-comments

43 Ken Ammi, "Atheist wars vs. Religious wars," *TrueFreeThinker* :http://truefreethinker.com/articles/atheist-wars-vs-religious-wars

44 Jill Pantozzi, "Raised by Wolves Is White, Gooey Nonsense," *Gizmodo*, October 2, 2020: https://www.gizmodo.com.au/2020/10/raised-by-wolves-is-white-gooey-nonsense

45 Ken Johnson, Th.D., *Ancient Post-Flood History*, p. 101

46 Samuel Spencer, "'Raised By Wolves' Ending Explained: Show Boss Breaks Down Season Finale," *Newsweek*, October 1, 2020: https://www.newsweek.com/raised-wolves-ending-explained-season-

finale-aaron-guzikowski-interview-hbo-max-1535319

[47] Samuel Spencer, "'Raised By Wolves' Ending Explained: Show Boss Breaks Down Season Finale," *Newsweek*, October 1, 2020: https://www.newsweek.com/raised-wolves-ending-explained-season-finale-aaron-guzikowski-interview-hbo-max-1535319

[48] Jennifer Vineyard, "'Raised by Wolves': Ridley Scott Explains That Monstrous Finale," *New York Times*, October 1, 2020: https://www.nytimes.com/2020/10/01/arts/television/raised-by-wolves-finale-ridley-scott.html

[49] Samuel Spencer, "'Raised By Wolves' Ending Explained: Show Boss Breaks Down Season Finale," *Newsweek*, October 1, 2020: https://www.newsweek.com/raised-wolves-ending-explained-season-finale-aaron-guzikowski-interview-hbo-max-1535319

[50] Samuel Spencer, "'Raised By Wolves' Ending Explained: Show Boss Breaks Down Season Finale," *Newsweek*, October 1, 2020: https://www.newsweek.com/raised-wolves-ending-explained-season-finale-aaron-guzikowski-interview-hbo-max-1535319

[51] Jennifer Vineyard, "'Raised by Wolves': Ridley Scott Explains That Monstrous Finale," *New York Times*, October 1, 2020: https://www.nytimes.com/2020/10/01/arts/television/raised-by-wolves-finale-ridley-scott.html

[52] Jennifer Vineyard, "'Raised by Wolves': Ridley Scott Explains That Monstrous Finale," *New York Times*, October 1, 2020: https://www.nytimes.com/2020/10/01/arts/television/raised-by-wolves-finale-ridley-scott.html

[53] Jill Pantozzi, "Raised by Wolves Is White, Gooey Nonsense," *Gizmodo*, October 2, 2020: https://www.gizmodo.com.au/2020/10/raised-by-wolves-is-white-gooey-nonsense

[54] Meghan O'Keefe, "'Raised by Wolves' Star Amanda Collin Reacts to That Insane Season 1 Finale: 'What the Actual F**k?'," *Decider*, October 1, 2020: https://decider.com/2020/10/01/raised-by-wolves-amanda-collin-mother-interview

[55] Meghan O'Keefe, "'Raised by Wolves' Star Amanda Collin Reacts to That Insane Season 1 Finale: 'What the Actual F**k?'," *Decider*, October 1, 2020: https://decider.com/2020/10/01/raised-by-wolves-amanda-collin-mother-interview

[56] Meghan O'Keefe, "'Raised by Wolves' Season 2 Theories That May (or May Not) Happen," *Decider*, Oct 14, 2020: https://decider.com/2020/10/14/raised-by-wolves-season-2-best-fan-theories

[57] TheBigLahey, "Raised by Wolves is heavily based off the religious

text The Book of Enoch and is about to get really weird," *Reddit*,
September, 2020 :
https://www.reddit.com/r/television/comments/iqouy3/raised_by_wolv
es_is_heavily_based_off_the

[58] Meghan O'Keefe, "'Raised by Wolves' Season 2 Theories That May
(or May Not) Happen," *Decider*, Oct 14, 2020:
https://decider.com/2020/10/14/raised-by-wolves-season-2-best-fan-
theories

[59] Mithra entry, *Encyclopedia Bitannica*:
https://www.britannica.com/topic/Mithra

[60] David Ulansey, "MITHRAISM: The Cosmic Mysteries of Mithras,"
Mysterium: http://www.mysterium.com/mithras.html

[61] "Mithras past-present-future," *Carnaval*:
http://www.carnaval.com/mithras

[62] "Mithras past-present-future," *Carnaval*:
http://www.carnaval.com/mithras

[63] Kenneth Grant, *Aleister Crowley and The Hidden God* (Skoob
Books, Great Britain, 1973), pp. 161-162

[64] Maev Kennedy, "Reconstructed Roman Temple of Mithras opens to
public in London
Visitors to new museum will uncover mystery cult of Mithras the bull
slayer in multi-sensory experience," *The Guardian*, November 8, 2017:
https://www.theguardian.com/science/2017/nov/08/reconstructed-
roman-temple-mithras-opens-public-bloomberg-hq

[65] Mithra entry, *Encyclopaedia Britannica*:
https://www.britannica.com/topic/Mithra

[66] Baphomet entry, *Wikipedia*: http://en.wikipedia.org/wiki/Baphomet

[67] Ken Ammi, "Burning Cross and El Zorro (…aster, that is)," *True
Free Thinker*: http://truefreethinker.com/articles/burning-cross-and-el-
zorro-%E2%80%A6aster

[68] Mithra entry, *Wikipedia*: https://en.wikipedia.org/wiki/Mithra

[69] Aleister Crowley, Mary Desti, Leila Waddell, and Hymenaeus Beta,
eds., *Magick: Liber ABA, Book Four, Parts I–IV* (York Beach, Me.: S.
Weiser)

[70] See John Carter, *Sex and Rockets: the Occult Life of Jack Parsons*
(USA: Feral House, 2005), pp. 151-153

[71] Aleister Crowley, *The Spirit of Solitude: an autohagiography:
subsequently re-Antichristened The Confessions of Aleister Crowley*
(London: Mandrake Press, 1929)

[72] James Patrick Holding, "Mithra vs Jesus," *Tektonics*:
https://tektonics.org/copycat/mithra.php

[73] That source was the following link when Holding first wrote the

---

article I am quoting as an appendix, but the site no longer hosts the article he referenced: http://www.pantheon.org/articles/a/anahita.html
[74] http://www.tektonics.org/books/palmersutrvw.php

Printed in Great Britain
by Amazon

80670184R00132